"With extraordinary detail and tender insight, Patricia Spranger traces the tracks of her past in an effort to understand the woman she has become today. *Second Chances* is an inspiring story that shows, if given the chance, it is possible to remake our lives and ourselves into something bigger and better than we ever thought possible."

Janice Gary, author of *Short Leash: A Memoir of Dog Walking and Deliverance.*

"These quiet, contemplative essays are studded with unexpected moments and astute insights, with lovely turns of phrase evoking the small dramas and dreams that make up a lifetime."

Catherine Clifford, former Self Magazine senior writer/ senior editor, national magazine writer, and contributor to the book, *Mommy Wars.*

"Spranger tells the stories of her life with a patient attention to individual words and details that spin the tales out seamlessly. I've watched her hold the attention of a writing group with just a first, rough draft. So imagine how her writing flows with the polish and perspective of time and the linking of individual stories to create a life."

Mary Carpenter, author of the middle-grade biography of Temple Grandin, *Rescued by a Cow and a Squeeze.*

Second Chances

Dear Beth,

It's p. nice to

know you.

Happy Drawbsging! 2022

Pat

Second Chances

FROM TRUCK STOP WAITRESS TO PSYCHOTHERAPIST

* * *

Patricia Spranger

ISBN-13: 9781530109357
ISBN-10: 1530109353

Table of Contents

For My Family, with Love

Foreword

* * *

WHEN I BEGAN TAKING WRITING classes at the Writer's Center in Bethesda, Maryland, over ten years ago, the idea of writing a book had never occurred to me. My goals had simply been to hone my writing skills in order to describe some of my life experiences for my children as clearly as possible so that they would come to know me as a complete person, not just their parent.

To my surprise, as the stack of pieces grew over time, I began to see cohesive threads weaving their way into a unified whole. My writing was not just an autobiographical recounting of events, but an explanation of how certain decisions I made led to pivotal turning points of my life, which afforded me more opportunities for personal growth and contentment. Having little else to go on, I had trusted my feelings and instincts to guide me out of unsatisfying situations toward more life satisfaction. I was willing to take certain risks, even with anxiety as a frequent companion, and to believe that I would be able to cope with whatever happened next.

In addition to writing this memoir for my children, I ended up writing it for myself, although I didn't know it at the time. The process of writing has helped me to gain insight and to make sense of my life, to understand why I left my marriage, and why I chose to become a psychotherapist.

It is my hope that people reading this book can find some of my experiences helpful to them as they walk along their path in life. Perhaps they can avoid some of the mistakes I made and profit from some of my successes. Most of all, I wish them the bravery to do what feels right and not be afraid of changing their mind if things don't pan out the first time. As one door of life closes, another one is ajar, ready to reveal new possibilities. We just need the courage to push it open and face what's on the other side. Life is full of second chances.

"Life's ups and downs provide windows of opportunity to determine your values and goals. Think of using all obstacles as stepping stones to build the life you want."

Marsha Sinetar

Part One
Shaky Beginnings

* * *

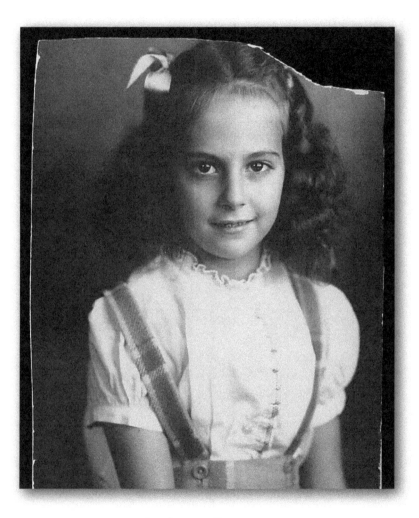

Iris Patricia Overstreet
Circa 1946

Going to the Lake

*   *   *

M Y FATHER WAS AGITATED THAT morning as he often was when waiting for other people, regardless of the reason. He paced back and forth in the house while sighing heavily. "Hurry up, let's go! Iris, aren't you ready yet?" he bellowed angrily through the house, but pointedly at my mother. He could hardly wait to get on the road to take a day off from his usual, ten-hour days at work. As the manager of a truck stop, he had a hard time finding reliable help to relieve him for a day. Since he allowed himself these Sunday family getaways only rarely, maybe once every three or four weeks in the summers of my childhood, he wanted to get in a full day. We couldn't afford to take real vacations, and he wanted to secure a good spot with a nice picnic table under a shade tree near the lake's sandy swimming area.

My sister Terry and I would be ready early, with bathing suits already on underneath our shorts and halter-tops. But Mom would still be working in the kitchen, putting the finishing touches on her deviled eggs, crunchy fried chicken, and velvety potato salad, our picnic favorites that we had all come to expect. The tantalizing aromas made our mouths water, even if we had just finished breakfast. Mom put a lot of thought into our provisions, trying to make everyone happy. Left up to Daddy, we'd be lucky to have a pack of hot dogs with white rolls for the day and one towel to share among us.

Mom often got upset with Daddy for rushing her and would snap back with "Well, Ben, if you did more to help, we could leave sooner!" We kids would cringe, hoping this angry exchange wouldn't escalate into another full blown marital skirmish to dash our plans for a fun day.

Our parents had heated arguments at times, but on lake days, they were usually able to restrain themselves. They seemed to enjoy spending a day at the lake as much as my sister and I. When she was mad at Daddy, Mom might give him the cold shoulder for the first part of the hour-long drive up to the lake, but eventually she would thaw and break the silence, at first by saying something to my sister or me like, "Oh, look at the pretty cows over on that hill", as we drove along the hot country roads. Daddy acted as if nothing had been wrong in the first place and already had the radio on, searching for base-ball scores.

Terry and I stayed hushed on the edge of the back seat of the car, slightly holding our breath. We didn't want to say anything to start an argument and disturb the tentative peace between our parents. We were cramped between fold-ing chairs, beach blankets, the large, round sweaty thermos jug with iced tea, and, most important, the picnic basket. A flowered, plastic shoulder bag held a bottle of Johnson's Baby Oil mixed with iodine to promote our tans, a Dell paperback mystery for Daddy, the latest Reader's Digest for Mom, mosquito spray, and a small first aid kit, mostly for my feet, which I frequently cut walking barefoot.

Our legs perspired where our thighs stuck to the hot vinyl seat, and we had to move gingerly so our skin wouldn't tear. Since there was no air conditioning back in the late 40's, we had the car windows open full blast when it was hot. When my parents lit up their cigarettes, the wind sometimes blew the ashes into our eyes. But with the windows closed, we'd almost suffocate from the cigarette smoke. I'd regularly get car sick, especially during the second half of the trip when the road got steep and windy, leading up to a gap in the mountains where the lake was. In fact, the place was called Cowan's Gap State Park, near Stone Mountain, located in southern Pennsylvania.

By the time we arrived and piled out of the car, everyone was so excited to see the clear, calm water of the lake, that miffs and moodiness were quickly forgotten. Oh, the smell of the place! The pungent pine mixed with musty decay of leaves held promise of a carefree day in this woodsy setting. The late morning air was still crisp and cool, the sandy white beach yet undisturbed by footprints. Bright sparkles danced so dazzlingly in wavy curves on the surface of the lake, that, at first, it hurt our eyes.

While our parents settled in under the shade tree to read, Terry and I ran for the water, but always stopped dead at its icy edge, shocked by the cold every time anew. The lake must have been fed by arctic reservoirs that stayed frigid all summer, regardless of the air temperature. We finally made it in, laughing and splashing each other, but kept glancing back to see if our parents were ready to join us. They both loved swimming and taught us how to swim as soon as we were out of diapers. The family pictures that showed our parents looking happy were usually taken at pools, beaches and lakes, at first as a couple alone, then with their first child, my sister, and finally with me, four years later. Mom and Daddy relaxed and played with us at the lake, which they rarely did at home where they were caught up in the work and worry of daily existence.

I loved watching my mother glide smoothly through the water, not making a splash, just like Esther Williams, a famous film star of the day. Daddy's strokes were clumsier, his big belly probably impeding his form. He liked to amuse himself by squirting water, fountain-like, up through his clasped hands, which he pumped together under the water. His aim was so good he could splash one of us at a distance of almost ten feet, usually catching us unawares and yielding peels of giggles.

Lunchtime at the picnic table saw voracious appetites, approving nods and satisfying grunts. We complimented Mom on her delicious food, hoping to erase any vestiges of her upset feelings from that morning. My favorite was her famous deviled eggs, the fillings with just the right touch of tanginess. Her secret was mixing in a few drops of vinegar with some yellow mustard and Hellman's Real Mayonnaise. No off-brands would do.

After lunch, Daddy would lean back in his lounge chair and doze off, his mystery story upside down on his large lap, which my mother referred to as his "bay window". Mom would sit with

Terry and me on our blanket by the water, all of us slathered with baby oil, while our food digested. In those days, people believed you'd get stomach cramps if you swam within an hour after eating. (I'd never met anyone this had happened to, but it was a strictly followed rule, nevertheless.) After waiting for what seemed like forever, when all danger of cramping had supposedly past, we'd bound back into the water to savor the rest of the day.

As the sun began to sink behind the trees in late afternoon and the crowd started to thin out, it was time to load up the car again and start home. None of us wanted to leave that peaceful place. Being outdoors all day had a soothing effect on us. My parents were smiling and agreeable, a mood we rarely experienced at home. But it didn't last long. After a few days back in their normal, stressful routines, the bickering would start again, in low rumbles at first, like a thunderstorm approaching slowly from the distant horizon, and then erupt in loud, scary clashes. My sister and I kept hoping, as kids often do, that things might change. We wanted the good feelings from the lake to follow us home and move in with us permanently.

If only our parents could have bottled the mellow effects of those Sundays at the lake, and taken frequent nips as needed, their relationship might have survived. I believe they loved each other, and tried hard to keep the marriage together, but maybe they really weren't suited for each other. Maybe their personalities were too different, or their expectations too discordant. But this much is true: I was witness to the times at the lake when they were able to get along, to share moments of contentment, to laugh with each other, and provide beautiful memories for all of us.

Iris Adelaide Love Overstreet
9-10-1915 to 11-23-1987

Illness

* * *

AS A CHILD, I WAS frequently ill. When I came down with flu or a fever, my mother nursed me with hot soups, mashed potatoes and tapioca pudding served on a tray she brought to my bed. To ease the phlegm in my chest, she'd make a mustard plaster, an age-old remedy to speed recovery, consisting of layers of muslin covered with warm mustard, that she had heated up on the stove until a test on the inside of her wrist confirmed the right temperature. She would spread the warm mustard evenly with a butter knife onto the cloth across my chest from my neck down to my belly button, careful not to miss any spots where the infection could hide. Then she'd cover me with thick towels to seal in the warmth of the preparation.

Mom was sure of herself when caretaking. I remember feeling instant relief as I breathed in the pungent mustard smell, which would help loosen the congestion and reduce the coughing fits that kept me awake at night. I felt the soothing heat seep down through the layers to my skin. "Umm, Mommy, that feels so good," I'd say. She'd reassure me in her slightly

Southern accent, "Well, I'm glad, honey. I'm sure you'll feel better soon. You rest now. I'll be downstairs if you need me." Her worried blue eyes would linger above me as she tucked the blankets in behind my shoulders.

Mustard plasters were a messy procedure, to be sure. I wonder how my mother dealt with the gooey, yellow pile of towels when she removed them from my chest after about an hour. As a young child of five, six, and seven, I never thought to ask her. Typically, she would submit herself to any household ordeal and chip away at it, uncomplainingly, until it was done.

Mom had a so-called modern, electric washer with an agitator in the basement of our two-story rental house in Frederick, but she still had to hand-crank the laundry through rollers to squeeze out the water. I loved handing her the wet pieces and hearing the satisfying squish while each piece of laundry descended as a thin, flat board from the wringer. Spin cycles hadn't been invented yet, not to mention automatic dryers, but at least she didn't have to use a scrub board on the edge of the bathtub anymore. After going through the wringer, each piece of laundry had to be vigorously shaken back from its board state into its original, recognizable shape. I felt proud handing Mom the clothespins as she hung up the laundry on a clothesline in the backyard. Sometimes she pretended not to see me sneak up on her from behind the large, flapping sheets, and squealed when I hollered, "Boo!"

As much as I hated being stuck inside and missing school, I loved getting my mother's full attention when I was sick. At those times I felt really special. She'd bring me little get-well presents from the store, like a comic book or crayons and a coloring book. Once, she cut a small hole in the end of an orange and showed me how to squeeze it while sucking out the juice. This method of drinking juice became a treat I looked forward to every time I was ill.

Mom had no formal education beyond high school, but she had a wealth of practical knowledge. I imagine that she learned the mustard plaster remedy growing up in the hills of Booie, North Carolina, probably from her mother who had learned it from her mother, and so on down the generations. Mom later taught me how to use other homespun remedies, like soothing tired eyes with cotton pads soaked in witch hazel, or rinsing my hair with diluted apple vinegar to make it really shine. Store-bought hair conditioner wasn't available yet. If the cake fell, or the potato salad was too salty, she knew how to camouflage the mistake. After a day of scrubbing floors, she'd soak in a tub of Epsom salts to soothe her tired back. She'd rig up a bowl of hot water with eucalyptus oil to inhale when her sinuses were blocked. She looked like a female sheik, her head covered with a white towel hanging down around the bowl.

Mom would have made a terrific nurse, if she had had a chance to go to college. When I hurt myself, she'd deftly bandage my scraped knee and could pull out the tiniest shard of glass from the bottom of my foot without flinching. But back in her day, growing up poor in a rural area as she did, there was little opportunity or encouragement for women to pursue a professional career. In later years, after one of the recurrent separations from Daddy, she was determined to better herself and went to night school to learn shorthand and typing. I can still see her at the kitchen table after supper, bent over her spiral notebook with pale, green pages, practicing the squiggly symbols for words commonly used in dictation. With a focused brow she would mouth the syllables as she drew the graceful flourishes repeatedly across the page.

Sometimes Mom would have me read a business letter from her assignment book out loud while she rendered it in shorthand. Afterwards, I'd hear her transcribing the letter to her small Corona typewriter. An occasional stop in her typing usually meant she couldn't decipher one of the shorthand symbols she'd written. "Gosh, darn it!" she'd shout – Mom rarely cursed in earnest. Then, hardly a minute later, "Hot dog!" when she had figured out the word and the rapid clattering would resume as she finished transcribing the letter.

I was impressed with her seemingly magical ability at shorthand, which later landed her several good jobs. She tried hard to please her bosses, and got upset when she made a mistake. She craved praise and approval from others. Normally soft-spoken, she often deferred to others, as if she didn't trust her own opinions. It was hard for her to speak up for herself.

I remember asking Mom questions about the world and life in general, to which she'd frequently answer apologetically, "Patsy, I really don't know," and the matter was dropped. I sensed her embarrassment in not knowing things. She'd sometimes suggest ways I could find the answers, like asking the teacher or going to the library, but she didn't actively help me. Our family did not own a set of encyclopedias, and there were no home computers yet. It wasn't until years later that I learned to research information and, most important, learned that there is no shame in not knowing something.

Although Mom couldn't teach me to speak up for myself, she did teach me many valuable skills, like penny-wise shopping, cooking from scratch, mending clothes and doing laundry. I was interested in all of these tasks, and helped her as soon as I was old enough to carry a bag, stir the pot, guide the needle and hold the iron. A patient teacher, she took bits of time from her busy routine of keeping house and making meals to show me what she knew. She kept our home tidy, but not obsessively so. She'd stop work by mid-afternoon to relax with a cup of coffee, a Pall Mall cigarette and the latest copy of Readers Digest in her easy chair before starting to fix supper.

When I grew older and doctors' prescriptions were more commonly used to treat the flu, the mustard plasters fortunately, or unfortunately, depending on how you looked at it, came to an end. This faster, cleaner way to treat illness was a godsend to my mother, I'm sure. She was working outside the home by then and seldom had time to give me her full attention anymore. But popping pills from a bottle could never compete with the soothing touch of her gentle hands.

As an adult, I understand that she was very busy, especially later as a single parent when she started working full time. She shouldered most of the responsibilities alone, paying the bulk of our expenses on her meager salary, because Daddy's child support payments were sporadic. She was often physically exhausted and emotionally drained at the end of the day.

Weekends had to be spent catching up on household chores, running errands, shopping and cooking. I'm amazed at how much she accomplished.

As a child, even though I understood that things had changed and she didn't have the same kind of time for me, I still longed for the old days when she played jacks or Old Maids with me, or took me to the playground, or packed a picnic lunch for just the two of us to take to the creek. I felt very special then, like I mattered most to her in the world. Of course, she still took care of me when I was sick, but I never got that same undivided attention from her again.

Learning to Read

*   *   *

THE EXCITEMENT OF LEARNING TO read compared to nothing I had experienced in my young life up until then. My first grade teacher, Mrs. Motter, had given me the key to a magic kingdom full of wondrous stories just waiting to be released. All I had to do was unravel the letters on the page into readable words by sounding them out just like she said.

I had turned six on April 16, 1946 and must have been at just the right stage of development to learn to read when school started in September. My parents, like most parents in those days, had not tried to teach me to read beforehand, because the whole point of first grade was to learn how to read. We weren't supposed to do it earlier, so that we all started on the same playing field. Actually, we might have found it unfair if some kids in the class had already known how to read. We were encouraged to recite the alphabet, maybe count to 100, and name the colors before first grade, but not much else.

At our school in Frederick, Maryland, we used a textbook with stories about two kids named Dick and Jane, and their dog, Spot. Dick and Jane roamed the neighborhood freely, doing a lot of looking and seeing, and, on the part of Spot, running and jumping. Dick would say something like, "Look, Jane, see Spot jump," and Jane would say, "Look, Dick, see Spot run". Most people of my generation know at least some Dick and Jane lines – we must have all had the same reading book in first grade – and refer to them with humor, but also much fondness.

I don't remember any mention of parents in the book, which may have been part of its appeal. The little vignettes were rather nonsensical at best, and very repetitive, but I loved them. I relished holding the book in my hands and breathing in the slightly musty odor of the pages. I sat in the front of the class, hoping to be called on to read, and was enthralled each time I unlocked the secrets of rows of letters to reveal words I understood.

Mrs. Motter was a kind and patient lady who urged each of us to trust ourselves. "You can do it." "Sound it out." "Good work." "See, you got it!" She saw each hesitation as an opportunity for encouragement, never a reason to criticize, and spent extra time with the children who didn't catch on right away. She had grey hair, a plump figure and twinkling eyes. I don't think she was married or had children of her own. She smiled frequently and made reading fun.

Suddenly, about mid-year, Mrs. Motter was absent and we got a substitute teacher, for what we thought, and hoped, would be a short time. This new teacher did her job well enough. She was friendly and took us through our routines, but lacked Mrs. Motter's special spark.

We didn't want to hurt her feelings, but after a few days, we started to ask when Mrs. Motter would be back.

At first, the substitute looked uncertain, like she wasn't sure how to answer. She said she didn't really know, that she would ask the principal, but then she never told us. After a couple of months, we finally learned that Mrs. Motter wasn't coming back after all, but we weren't told why. We were left hanging, to imagine her retired, or sick, or dead, but never knowing the truth.

In those times, adults would whisper in low tones around children when bad things happened, as if we couldn't handle the sadness that tragedy sometimes brings. Perhaps they just wanted to protect us, but we had been sad anyway since Mrs. Motter left our midst and caused a void no one else could fill. The adults may have meant well, but I think not knowing her condition made it worse for us. We might have been able to do something, like visit her, send flowers, or at least write a card – some way to wish her well, or say good-bye. We could have let her know how much she had meant to us, which might have eased her pain. She must have missed us, too, after all, and may have welcomed our attention.

I think children should be told the truth, in words they can understand, and be encouraged to express their feelings about it. Knowing the truth also helps them accept reality and put closure to the situation, rather than be left wondering what happened. To this day, there is a tiny ache in my heart whenever I think about the wonderful lady who taught me how to read.

Martha Lewis Johnson Overstreet
3-16-1878 to 5-16-1946

Robert Pleasant Overstreet
7-10-1869 to 7-10-1949

Visiting My Father's Family

*   *   *

Wʜᴇɴ I ᴡᴀs ʏᴏᴜɴɢ, I believed that most of my relatives on my father's side fit my idea of how a stable and contented family should be. His mother and three sisters were down to earth, friendly and happy to talk to you for hours about what they had for lunch, who they saw at the drug store, or what kind of hat their neighbor wore to church last Sunday. Their slow, easy small talk was somewhat boring to me, yet comforting in a way, lending a sense of normalcy and predictability to our visits, which was often lacking in our family.

Even though I was prone to carsickness, I always looked forward to our trips to my grandparents' house. My parents, my sister Terry and I would make the six- or seven-hour drive from Maryland to Roanoke, Virginia, several times a year, most certainly for Thanksgiving and Christmas, plus at least one other time, usually in summer. I would fight, and not always win, the battle of nausea on the way. In those days, the roads were hilly and winding over the Blue Ridge Mountains, before huge Caterpillars sliced their way through the pristine blue-green of the mountaintops to build modern roads. To make matters worse, the smoke of my parents' cigarettes made my sister and me dizzy on the back seat of the car. Our pleas for them to stop smoking, at least for the trip, fell on deaf ears, but we didn't want to upset them by complaining too much. We were happy any time they weren't bickering.

Long and cramped as the drive was, it was worth it. The anticipation of playing with my cousins, Nancy and Grover, who were both around my age, eating grandma's scrumptious food and sleeping under cozy eiderdowns kept me going. As the Nehi soda ads on giant billboards got more frequent along the way, I took heart that we were getting closer to our destination. Soon we'd stop for a meal, and my sister and I would be allowed to order Dr. Peppers, a type of soda not yet sold in the north. We'd eat pork barbeque or something served with grits to celebrate having crossed into the real Dixieland. Even though, technically, Maryland was a southern state, it was a mish-mash of allegiances. After several years of driving to Roanoke, I had memorized the important points along the way: the courthouse in Winchester, Virginia, with its sculpture of a big red apple in front; the Luray caverns; Stuckeys' pecan shops; and, at last, Natural Bridge, the landmark signaling the last leg of our trip.

When we finally arrived, bedraggled but excited, the large family would engulf us on the front porch, hugging and smooching, and making us feel at home. My cousins and my three aunts, Louise, Ruby and Virginia with their spouses, would have already descended on my grandparents' house before our arrival. Terry and I would chuckle when they said "Y'all" this and "Y'all" that, and would try to imitate their Southern accent. By the third day at the latest, we'd be speaking "Southern," too. It was that contagious.

My parents were on their best behavior during these visits, a welcome calm in their normally agitated relationship. Mom busied herself with her sisters-in-law helping grandma in the kitchen, seeming more at ease with herself around them. A bit shy by nature, she wasn't very sociable at home, where she didn't know many people. Daddy sat with the men, commenting on the weather or betting who would win the next ballgame. He looked comfortable in the home where he had grown up. It was a modest, two-story frame house with a front porch full of gliders and rockers for socializing, especially after dinner.

Neighbors would stop by on their evening walks and chit-chat from the sidewalk with one foot on the front step, catching up on the local news: "How's that back of yours, Ruby?" "Did you hear about old Mr. Smith falling down the steps?" "I understand First Baptist has a new pastor." I wished we had front porches at the places we lived and neighbors that knew each other so well.

My grandfather was somewhat standoffish. He'd sit in his rocking chair, usually unsmiling, and observe the proceedings from a distance. He, like my grandmother, always looked exhausted, but she made an effort to make everyone feel welcome. He had worked hard on the railroad all his life for a meager salary and had raised six kids, one of whom, Bill, had Down's syndrome. Aside from an occasional nod, Bill rarely joined in the conversation. He sometimes muttered under his breath, or swirled a long string around in circles, but never caused any trouble. He was generally quiet, and had always lived at home. In those days, there were no programs yet for people with special needs. We kids didn't interact with him much, but accepted him as part of the family.

Only one of my father's siblings, his older brother Bob, was usually missing from these get-togethers. Uncle Bob was the only college-educated member of the family. According to my father, there was too little money for my grandparents to send both boys to college, so he went to a vocational school to learn welding. Since that time, there seemed to have been ongoing friction between my father and my uncle that caused, or perhaps deepened, an existing rift between them.

One time on our way home from a long trip, we stopped at my Uncle Bob's house late at night with the plan of spending the night there and continuing on the next day. He and his wife Francis welcomed us at the door. We hadn't seen them for a long time. Due to the late hour, Terry and I were whisked off to bed, where we promptly fell asleep. The next thing I knew, I awoke with a start to the sound of my father and his brother screaming at each other in the living room, and my mother's shaky voice telling us to get up because we were leaving. It was hard waking up from a deep sleep in a warm bed and then going out into the cold car in the dark of night. The adults' angry faces scared and confused me. Everything had seemed fine when we first arrived. I never found out what had transpired between the brothers, but, to my knowledge, they never spoke again after that.

Most of my father's family, however, got along very well and looked forward to our get-togethers. Just getting meals for that crowd was quite an accomplishment. We had to set the table for around twenty people, which meant putting mismatched tables together into a big, uneven square, which practically filled the dining room. The enticing aromas of fried chicken and freshly baked pies coming from the kitchen spurred everyone to help get dinner ready. Tasks were divvied up, with some people taking the biscuits out of my grandmother's wood-fired cook stove, others making the gravy, or dishing up the greens, mashing the potatoes, or stoking the coal stove to keep us warm through dinner. Unlike at our house, we bowed our heads and said grace before eating, and waited until everyone's plate was served from the many bowls and platters passed around the table before taking a bite.

Finally, a chorus of ahs and lip-smacking rose up from the table, followed by a tinny orchestra of scraping forks and knives until the last person was stuffed and practically every serving dish was empty. We children had to finish our greens if we wanted dessert. There were pies of every imaginable fruit, depending on the season, but always pumpkin and mincemeat for the holidays and cherry and apple in the summer. My aunts, who either grew the fruit themselves, or harvested it from my grandfather's backyard trees and bushes, could have opened a bakery with their talent. My favorite was apple pie, filled with countless layers of tangy, ripe slices mixed with just the right amount of cinnamon and brown sugar to create a tongue's delight.

After dinner, everyone would sit around the living room, warmed by the stove in winter, or on the porch, cooled by the balmy breeze in summer, and talk until bedtime. My favorite cousin Nancy and I would play Old Maids or Parcheesi on the floor, with one ear on the adults' conversation. I envied her for her parents who looked at each other lovingly and often laughed together. They joked around but always treated each other with respect. We once found a jar of Vaseline in their nightstand and smirked about what it was used for. Nancy's family appeared to be so happy. I wished our family could be more like theirs. Sometimes my parents would get along for a while, but I was constantly on edge waiting for the next storm to brew.

One thing I didn't like about our visits was that we had to go to church with our relatives on Sunday. I liked donning my frilly dress and paten leather shoes for the occasion, but I found it hard to sit still on the hard, wooden pews during the long sermon. The pastor scared me when he preached that anyone not accepting Jesus Christ as their Savior could not enter the "kingdom of heaven." Something about that belief didn't make sense to me, even as a young child. After all, our next-door neighbors in Frederick were Jewish and very good friends of ours for the time that we lived on North Market Street. Their daughter Rosie and I often played hide-and-go-seek together or dressed up as Gypsies at Halloween. How could they be refused heaven just because they had a different religion? Even though my parents considered our family Christians, we rarely went to church. Did that mean we wouldn't get to heaven?

When I asked my parents about this, they smiled at me indulgently but didn't say much to allay my fears.

At bedtime in winter at my grandparents' house, Nancy and I would creep up the cold stairs into the freezing bedroom where we shared a big bed towering with covers to keep us warm. There was no central heating, only a few vents cut into the ceiling downstairs to let some heat upstairs. Still, the floor was so icy that we waited to take off our socks until we were in bed. Under the bed there was a bedpan with a lid, in case we had to go to the bathroom during the night. I hated having to use it, because the rim of the porcelain pan would shock my warm bottom. Indoor plumbing hadn't yet arrived at my grandparents' house.

Nancy and I would lie awake telling each other stories, giggling so loud at times that my grandfather would yell at us through the wall to be quiet. Once, when he apparently had had enough of our noise, he stormed in and smacked my behind so hard I almost cried. I was shocked. Even though I had always been leery of him, I never thought he would hit me. My parents never hit me at home. I didn't tell them about the incident, for fear they might blame me for bothering him. From then on, I decided to make a big circle around my grandfather. At times, though, he could be nice, especially when he gave us peppermint candy kept in the top drawer of his dresser.

Saying good-bye was always hard when our visits came to an end. I knew I would miss playing with my cousins, but most of all I would miss the peaceful atmosphere of the family gathering. I longed to hold on to this safe nest, but knew it wasn't to be. Our family was different and I knew when we returned home, the routine of my parents' arguments would resume. Anything – a comment or complaint - could set one of them off. This was our "normal." This realization made me unhappy, yet I had no choice but to try to accept it and stay out of my parents' way.

The memory of these enjoyable visits with my relatives at my grandparents' house gave me hope that family life, although never perfect, could be more harmonious. Having watched some of my own relatives accomplish this, I believed it could be possible for me, too, one day. At least I was armed with the knowledge of some positive ingredients that go into a happy family, not just the negative ones that made for an unhappy one.

Middletown Farm

✳ ✳ ✳

WHEN I WAS SEVEN YEARS old, we lived as tenants on the second floor of a two-story frame house on a farm a few miles outside of Middletown, Maryland. Asthma had forced my father to leave his job as a welder, because the fumes made him cough. I watched him in action once at his job in a garage, welding broken metal parts together, as sparks and bluish smoke rose around his helmeted head. A strange, sour odor stung my nostrils and chest, making me want to gag. And I had healthy lungs. No wonder my father had to change jobs, but it meant earning less money, and, since rent was cheaper in the country than in Frederick, my parents had decided to move.

The farm was close enough for my father to commute to his new venture in Frederick, selling kitchen appliances in a small shop that he leased. Much to Mom's dismay, we couldn't afford to rent a place right in Middletown itself. She didn't dislike the country, but preferred "living in civilization", which to her meant in an urban area. However, she did her best to adapt to country life. She did particularly well in getting my sister and me to the school bus every morning. She woke us on time and had breakfast ready, but we dragged our feet. We never actually missed the bus, but every day was a mad dash out the door when we heard the screeching brakes of the yellow bus coming down the hill towards the top of our drive. Luckily, the driver was a patient man. He may also have chuckled to himself, watching us struggle with our schoolbooks and lunch boxes, half in and half out of our coats as we raced to meet him, afraid he'd leave without us.

One drawback of this cheaper rental was that we had to share a bathroom with the other tenants on our same floor. From our kitchen I could peer around a flimsy curtain through an interior window for a clear view into the bathroom. When their little boys around my age took a bath, I used to spy on them, curious to see what they had for private parts. Had she known, my mother would have been upset with me for acting in an unladylike manner, whereas my father would probably have chalked up my behavior to curiosity and shrugged his shoulders. When we bathed, our neighbors could not see us, as there was no window on their side. My mother didn't like the idea of sharing such an intimate space with other people and always scrubbed the tub hard with Ajax before we used it.

Roaming around outdoors, I loved the freedom of wide open spaces and was thrilled to see all the farm animals up close: fat hogs, milk cows and laying hens that I had seen mostly in picture books up until then. On weekends and after school, I visited them regularly, but I made a big arc around a ferocious looking bull they kept in a separate field. I'd been told that my maternal grandfather had been gored to death by a bull in North Carolina when my mother was a little girl.

We must have inherited a cat with the section of the house we occupied, because I'm sure we didn't bring one with us. Most of our previous rentals didn't allow pets. This cat was highly pregnant and soon delivered her kittens on a pile of shoes at the bottom of one of our closets. As she licked her wet newborns clean, they squirmed around each other, eyes tightly shut, vying for the best position at her teats. My heart warmed at the sight of these tiny creatures fresh from their mother's womb.

Death was as natural as birth on the farm. Again, it was something I knew about, but had never witnessed first hand. One day, I was outside making my rounds as usual to check on the animals, when I suddenly came across an open barn door. Looking inside, I winced at a large, dead hog hanging upside down by its hindquarters on steel hooks, its bloody entrails splattered on the ground. I thought I recognized him from my trips through the hog pen, and stopped short. It was shocking to see the lifeless animal in such a position. I was sad for him and embarrassed, as if I had walked in on something very private, and had seen him in a way he didn't want to be seen. I felt repulsed, yet fascinated, wanting to run, but not able to stop staring.

This bloodstained sight engrossed me, even as the horror of death sank in. I had seen dead animals before, mostly on the side of the road after being hit by a car. I may have felt sorry for them in general, but I had no personal relationship with them and wasn't affected for long. Also, looking out of the window of a car, there was usually some warning of a lump of something ahead, allowing time to look away. This hog had been part of my idyllic view of farm life and belonged in my daily routine of greeting the animals. It was startling to find him hanging there, motionless. My stomach turned as I quickly left the place.

Later that day, I went to the farmer's house to watch his wife working in her kitchen, which was one of my favorite activities. Oftentimes, she'd be canning or baking food, which produced such delectable aromas that I often asked for a taste. She was usually smiling and chatty, but this day was different. She opened the door with a scowl on her face and said, "Come on in, Patsy. Don't mind me." She pushed her stringy hair back from her sweaty brow and said, "I'm just upset because slaughtering day is so much work. The worst part is making sausage. It's such a messy job. I hate it!" She was moving about the hot kitchen abruptly, stern faced and heavy footed, clattering strange utensils that I had never seen before: odd-shaped gutting knives, sharp cleavers and a meat grinder.

Instead of the enticing smells I was used to, offensive odors rose up from large pots boiling on her stove. Cautiously, I looked under the lids at the swirling parts bubbling to the surface. As I detected an ear, then a hoof and an eye, I realized that this must be the slaughtered hog I had seen hanging in the barn. I backed away from the stove wanting to leave, but my curiosity overcame my queasiness, and I sat down at a safe distance to watch. I'd never seen, nor ever thought about, how sausage was made, although I had eaten it many times with scrambled eggs and biscuits for breakfast.

When the pieces - except for the hooves, which she put aside to pickle - were tender and had cooled sufficiently, the woman skinned, scraped and chopped them, then ground them all together with spices into a huge, vat-like container. Some of the pulpy globs slopped over the rim, smeared the table and slid to the floor. At that moment, her kitchen reminded me of the scene of slaughter from that morning, causing the same nausea to turn my stomach. Finally, she stuffed the mass into pre-cut lengths of the hog's intestines, which she had already cleaned to use for casing. As fatty juice ran down her hands and dripped onto her apron, she sighed as if resigned. I sympathized with her, but was relieved that she didn't ask me to help.

Across the kitchen I could see that the chops and loins had already been packed in cellophane and labeled for the freezer. They reminded me of the neatly wrapped portions of meat my mother bought at the grocery store, where the pieces were wiped clean and positioned on a cottony pad to absorb any unappetizing blood on the underside. Even the sausage came in cute little links with a smiling hog on the wrapper and no trace of blood. Before this experience, I had enjoyed the spicy kick that sausage gave to our breakfast, innocent as I was of the disgusting sausage making process.

When the last piece of meat was tied and stored, I went home. It was around dinnertime, when I would normally be ravenous after a day of adventure on the farm. This day, however, I wasn't hungry and only picked at my food, avoiding the meat on my plate. My parents asked me what was the matter, but I didn't know how to put it into words. I was afraid they might laugh at my reaction to the slaughter. After all, I had eaten meat all my life. But unwrapping a neat portion of meat from the butcher to cook for a meal is a far cry from having known the particular animal and seen him cut to pieces. I felt guilty about the hog's fate, and vowed to myself never to eat meat, especially sausage, again.

This promise didn't last very long. Ours was a meat eating family. Meals were usually built around the kind of meat on the menu, like beef, pork or poultry. Regulars were meat loaf, pork chops, pot roast and fried chicken. Only very occasionally did we have spaghetti and meatballs and never pizza. Italian food had not really caught on yet. We seldom had seafood either, unless a friend of my father's happened to land a trout from the nearby river. On the rare occasions when we ate out, and always at their favorite restaurant, the Peter Pan Inn, my parents would order big T-bone steaks.

I'm sure if I had ever tried to stop eating meat, my father would have made a big stink about it. He might have said that animals were raised to be slaughtered, and that I should "thank the Good Lord" for what He provided us. At the very least, he might have accused me of trying to be difficult. He would certainly have told me to stop the foolishness and finish the nice dinner that my mother had made for me.

Mother, on the other hand, might have inquired why I didn't want to eat meat. She would have sympathized with my feelings about slaughtering animals, but she would have voiced some concern about my getting enough protein. She may have hoped that I was going through some kind of phase that would soon pass.

My sister Terry probably would have voted to let me go without meat if I wanted. She would have wondered what the harm in that could be. She might have added that she learned about healthy vegetables and grains in school that provided enough nutrition. She may even have elected to go meatless with me.

As it turned out, none of this happened because I didn't try to avoid meat for long, at least not long enough for anyone to notice. Meat smelled so good sizzling in the pan, and Mom always cooked it just right, especially my favorite, cheeseburgers. I felt a little guilty, but only for a short time, and from then on, I was careful to avoid the parts of the farm where I thought more slaughtering could be done.

Nowadays, I still eat meat regularly, but I try to choose free range and organic meat whenever possible. Even though the animals are still slaughtered, I trust that it's done more humanely, and I assuage my conscience with the thought of the animals having lived happier lives for having been sheltered and fed regularly. I like vegetarian food, which is more abundant and available these days, but I think it's hard to get all the nutrients, especially protein, in a balanced way without meat. I'd have to learn how to do it properly. Besides, every now and then I get an irresistible yen for a fat, juicy turkey burger covered with mustard.

If I had to slaughter the animals myself, I'm sure I'd be a vegetarian, because I can't imagine killing anything larger than a mouse. While I can't pretend not to know how the meat reaches my plate, I try not to think about it. Yet, the upsetting spectacle of that dead hog hanging on a hook still lingers with me after all these years. I see no real way out of these conflicted feelings, but I try to accept my meager compromise of trying to eat less meat, and supporting groups that foster humane treatment of farm animals.

Next-door Neighbors

*   *   *

WHEN I WAS IN THIRD grade, my parents, my sister and I lived in an apartment above a tobacco shop on Patrick Street in Frederick, Maryland. I remember smelling some of the sweet cigar smoke every now and then and wondering what kind of people smoked them. My mother smoked Pall Malls. My father smoked Camel cigarettes without filters.

Across the alley on the same side of the street was a funeral home. The owners had two magnificent, large boxers that they kept out back in a cage with chain-link fencing and a cement floor. I was afraid to pet them, but I would go close to the cage and talk to them sometimes when the owner was around. He fed them every day and gave them treats. I'd watch him hose down the cage regularly. I never saw him walk the dogs, but I believe he drove them somewhere to let them run. The dogs were not allowed inside the house.

Their house had two stories, a downstairs for the business and an upstairs where they lived. When there was a funeral, I'd see the mourners going in and out of the front door and a black hearse parked out back near the dogs' cage. I always wondered what went on in the back room where the director worked. The blinds were drawn shut, so I couldn't peek inside. What did he do with the bodies to prepare them? He seemed to work by himself, as I never saw any assistants around.

As an eight-year-old girl, the thought of being alone with a dead body made me shudder. I thought the man must be weird somehow, yet he seemed friendly enough whenever I saw him, and he treated his dogs well. Surely an animal lover must be a good person, I reasoned.

One day the man's wife was at the front door sweeping their stoop. When she saw me playing hopscotch on the sidewalk, she invited me to come upstairs with her for some Christmas cookies she had just baked. I had never been inside a funeral parlor before. I stepped gingerly into the hallway, and looked wide-eyed into the alcoves where I assumed caskets would normally be set up for viewing. Luckily, there were none on that day, and I breathed more easily. Still, I followed the lady as closely as possible as she took me upstairs to their apartment.

The tantalizing aroma of freshly baked cookies greeted us at the door. The kitchen was filled with homemade delights on every surface. I had never seen such an assortment, some with sparkling green sugar on top, others with powdered "snow," some with chopped nuts and candied cherries, all cut out with special holiday cutters in the shape of snowflakes, pine trees, and Santa Clauses. They were still warm, and tasted delicious with the glass of milk she offered me. She asked me about my family and school, and what I liked to do. I felt comfortable, and chatted more openly with her than I did with most people I had just met.

I was intrigued with the piano in their living room. When I told her I wanted to learn to play the piano, she pulled out some beginner's lesson books and proceeded to explain the keyboard and the fingering to me. She made me feel special. I was thrilled and took to it easily, playing a few simple pieces like "Three Blind Mice" after a short while. When it came time for me to go home, she said I could come over any time to practice the piano. I thanked her and she showed me to the door. Even though I knew there was no one downstairs, I felt nervous walking down the steps by myself, but that was the only way to the front door. If anyone had asked me if I believed in ghosts, I would have said certainly not. But the heavy, purple drapes and thickly carpeted rooms of the funeral parlor emitted a certain eeriness nevertheless.

Every few weeks, I visited the neighbor lady to practice the piano and enjoy her seemingly endless supply of cookies. She was very nice and always welcomed me with a big "Hello, Patsy!" Her husband was usually downstairs at work. Part of me looked forward to these visits, but part of me dreaded passing through the hallway within view of the areas where bodies were sometimes laid out. I would open the front door cautiously and tiptoe across the foyer towards the stairs, hoping no bodies were there. At first I tried not looking towards the alcoves, but my curiosity got the better of me. When a dead person was in one of the viewing rooms, I held my breath and ran up the steps. It wasn't so bad if mourners were around the casket to block my view, but I usually went right after school, when no one was there but me.

I don't know what I was afraid of. I had seen my grandmother in an open casket in the parlor of her house when I was six. I knew dead people couldn't hurt me, so I was too embarrassed to ask the lady to meet me at the front door and walk upstairs with me. I also expected myself to conquer my fear, or at least manage it better as I became more familiar with the place. But the bodies looked so strange, like porcelain mannequins with their eyes closed, the men dressed in fine suits and ties, and the women in silk blouses, usually with a bow tied at the neck. Their paleness shone through the powdery makeup, giving a surreal appearance that frightened me. Their lips seemed pressed together in an unnatural expression. I never got used to the sight.

One Saturday, I was playing outdoors when suddenly I heard my sister Terry screaming. She and our parents had been upstairs in our apartment when I went out. Everything had seemed all right then. I wondered what had happened and had started upstairs to our apartment to investigate when Terry ran past me with my red-faced father chasing her, and yelling, "Come back here!" I had never known Terry to go over to the neighbors' before, but she ran inside the funeral home and up the stairs, trying to escape my father's wrath. I ran after them, crying, "What's wrong?"

I knew Terry must have done something to upset Daddy. The two of them were like oil and water at times, and had frequent arguments, but this seemed worse than usual. Mother also rushed in, pleading with Daddy to calm down, but he paid her no mind. The funeral director and his wife must have been shocked to see our whole family running into their place. I was scared, hoping in vain that Terry could get away from my father, but she had run into one of the back storage rooms, tripped and fallen down, and was now trapped in a corner. The loud ruckus caused the dogs to start barking out back. The man and his wife stood in the hallway outside of the room, aghast. I was praying that they would do something to intervene, but they remained silent as my father removed his belt.

Holding Terry down with his free hand, my father flogged her bare legs as hard as he could. "I'm sick of your disobedience! This will teach you a lesson!" he bellowed.

I sobbed, "Daddy, please stop!" as my mother tried to pull him away from my sister. I watched in horror as he whipped her legs, her back, and her arms.

Terry tried to protect herself with her hands, but it was futile. At thirteen years old, she was no match for a grown man. Finally, after his rage was spent, he told her to get up and go home. Terry was crying so hard she could hardly walk. Mother and I supported her on both sides, as we headed towards the door. The neighbors mumbled something, as if to ask if Terry was all right, but took no action to assist her. Mother helped Terry down the stairs, amid apologies to the neighbors for the disturbance.

There had been no one on view downstairs that day. If there had been, the incident might not have occurred. Or, if anyone had been in the funeral parlor on business, for example, perhaps my father would have curbed his wrath. I later learned the reason for my father's anger. My sister had broken several of his rules in close succession: She had used forbidden make-up, broken curfew, and, worst of all, had used his straight edge razor again to shave her legs.

Luckily, the belt's blows had not drawn blood, but the large, red welts all over Terry's body could be seen for a week, as she tended to have very pale, sensitive skin. My mother was outraged over the beating and wouldn't speak to my father for days. She told him he had gone too far this time. Once his anger subsided, I think he realized it, too. As far as I know, he never lost control of his temper like that again, but his outburst left me feeling uneasy around him for a long time.

The incident also changed how I felt about the kindly neighbor lady and her husband. In those days, the late 1940's, outsiders were hesitant to get involved in other people's family issues, be it child discipline or marital strife. These personal matters were thought to be private, no one else's business, and were to be handled within the family unit. In essence, parents were allowed to treat their kids any way they saw fit. Child abuse laws were practically non-existent.

As a child, I didn't know about these cultural mores. All I knew was that the neighbors had let my sister down and had not stepped in to stop the violence. I had thought they were trustworthy people, but they stood by and watched my sister being beaten. I left their house feeling confused and disillusioned. I don't think I ever went back there, partly because of embarrassment, but mostly because of the breach of trust I felt towards them.

Every time I go to a funeral or pass by a funeral home, I remember those neighbors and that traumatic afternoon. I wonder how different it would have been for all of us if the funeral director and his wife had stepped in and had had the courage to get involved.

Halloween

* * *

AFTER A PARTICULARLY FIERCE ARGUMENT with my father, my mother took my sister and me to Milwaukee to live with my grandmother Mildred and my cousin Donnie in Mildred's high-rise apartment for a while. At her request we didn't call her grandmother, because the term made her feel old. It wasn't clear whether we would be returning to Maryland, or staying indefinitely, depending on how things developed during the separation. I wasn't privy to what had happened between my parents and didn't dare ask my mother, since she was so upset. At such times, I thought it best to keep quiet and busy myself with my toys, like jacks or pick-up sticks, and keep my worries to myself.

Going north to Mildred's place was an uncertain adventure, which both excited and scared me. I wondered how we would manage without my father, and if and when we'd hear from him again. I wish my mother had given me some reassurances, but she probably didn't know herself what was going to happen and didn't realize I was feeling anxious about it. I've never blamed my parents for what they did or didn't do for me while I was growing up, because, given the knowledge and resources they had at the time, I think they did the best they could.

In Milwaukee I was outdoors most of the time. If no one was available to play with, I'd sometimes tool around in alleys or abandoned lots on my bike, looking for empty soda bottles to return to the store for the two-cent deposit, with which I'd buy myself candy or Bazooka bubble gum. Money was very tight. I can remember Mildred counting out quarters on the kitchen table to see if there was enough to buy both bread and milk. I would help search under the living room cushions for lost coins and sometimes contributed my bottle refund money to the cause.

In those days, most parents weren't big on supervision, believing that kids belonged outside in the fresh air, running around playing freely. However, Terry disliked playing outdoors, where the heat and mosquitoes bothered her. She preferred the more temperate confines of the house, sketching fashion clothes or doing her nails, and Mom didn't push the issue. After Terry had recovered from a mild case of polio as a young child, the doctor had warned my parents that she would probably be a very sensitive person from then on. His comment made them treat her with kid gloves at times, which didn't help her self-confidence.

Back then, there was no such thing as "play dates" per se, but random pick-up games. When there were other kids outside, I played cops and robbers or cowboys and Indians with them, taking turns being the bad guys and using vines and sticks for ropes and guns. We girls would sometimes play with our dolls, mothering them with cooing sounds while pushing them in miniatures carriages. My favorite dolly was one that could actually drink from a bottle and pee-pee through a hole between her legs. I was delighted when she wet her diaper and I got to change her like a real mommy, being careful not to prick her with the safety pins. I even sprinkled talcum powder on her behind so she wouldn't get diaper rash.

Sometimes I went exploring on my own in a park or any patch of woods I could find and stuff my pockets with pine-cones, mossy rocks or wild flowers. I also loved to swing from the monkey bars at the school playground after everyone had gone home. Pretending I was a star athlete, I'd do front and back flips on a parallel bar for the tickle thrill in my tummy as the wind whooshed past my ears, or just hang upside down for the head-rush. From about eight years old I wasn't expected home until suppertime, or sundown, whichever came first.

That Halloween, I went trick-or-treating with my cousin Donnie, who was three years older. My mother had asked him to keep an eye on me, since I was only eight at the time and this was a big city. I felt flattered to go with him, but I doubt if he felt the same about me, surely much preferring to go with his friends, but good-natured as he was, he didn't complain.

It was early evening, just after dark, with hoards of cos-tumed kids streaming down the streets, in and out of apart-ment buildings, looking for sweet loot. Ghosts and devils, witches and fairies, sparkling or menacing, all lusted after free candy to be had for the asking. I was thrilled to be out with the big kids. After a while of trick-or-treating together, somehow Donnie and I got separated, but by then I knew the ropes and continued on confidently, going door-to-door in the apartment buildings alone.

My eyes got bigger and bigger as my goody bag filled up with more candy than I had ever had at one time. Even some of my favorites were in my bag: Tootsie Rolls, Babe Ruth bars, Necco Wafers, Hershey's chocolate, candy corn and The Three Musketeers. As if in a greedy frenzy, I had no thought of stopping, even when I noticed the groups of kids had started to thin out. Also, the attention I was getting from the people answering their doors was enticing. They exclaimed about my Gypsy costume, which I had put together with a peasant blouse and a long, scarlet skirt and cinch belt from Mildred's closet, topped off with her colorful scarves and beads. We couldn't afford store-bought costumes, but I didn't mind. It was more fun making my own costume anyway. With my mother's make-up I had carefully outlined my dark brown eyes with black pencil and mascara, swirled my cheeks with rouge and applied her reddest lipstick for exotic effect.

Not wanting to miss any apartment, I worked systematically through each apartment building on the block, taking the elevator to the top floor and beginning at the end of the hallway of each floor. After ringing the doorbell expectantly, I could hardly wait to say the magic words. Most people were friendly and gave generously and I was thrilled to see my bag bulging, so heavy now that I could hardly carry it. In my eagerness to collect more and more candy, I lost track of time until one lady commented that I was "out late for a little girl." When I noticed that there were no other trick-or-treaters around the hallways, I scurried home with a clutch of fear in my throat, both sensing my isolation and worrying that my mother would scold me.

When I got home, Mother asked me where I'd been so long, but seemed satisfied when I answered, "Out trick-or-treating. Look what I got!" She must have assumed that Donnie had dropped me off and was staying out later with his friends. If she had known where I'd been alone, I'm sure she would have been aghast.

Thinking back, I was lucky that nothing bad happened to me that evening. I could have been molested or abducted by any of those strangers behind closed doors. Why was I spared when some others doing the same innocent things have been treated brutally? Maybe the random finger of tragedy was busy elsewhere in the city that night. Maybe a guardian angel was perched on my shoulder. Whatever may have been the case, I am thankful that my naïve trust in people was safeguarded and my curiosity and yen for adventure remained in tact. Yet, it could easily have been otherwise.

I wonder if our fate is pre-determined or whether many of life's happenings result from pure accident, being in the right or wrong place at the right or wrong time. Although I want to believe that we control much of our life's path by the choices we make – and I'm sure we do at times – sometimes, there seems to be no rhyme or reason to it. Whatever the answers are, they will remain a mystery to me. My only real choice is to accept this fact, and try to live each day to its fullest and savor every pleasant moment.

Phoenix Adventures

*   *   *

MY PARENTS CONTINUED TO HAVE problems in their marriage over the years, prompting my father's angry outbursts and my mother's tearful withdrawals. Part of my father's irritability must have stemmed from the chronic cough and difficulty breathing caused by his asthma. No wonder he was moody. I remember seeing him hunched over the kitchen table, coughing uncontrollably into a handkerchief, red-faced, wheezing and unable to speak. He would gasp for breath in between coughing fits. Having had whooping cough when I was seven years old, I could sympathize with him. The sensation of not getting enough air had been terrifying for me. When I'd ask Daddy if he was all right, he could only wave me away with his free hand. He used some kind of throat spray, which didn't help much. Medicines for asthma weren't very effective back then.

So when Daddy's doctor suggested he move away from the east coast to a drier climate to ease his condition, Daddy jumped right on it. I don't know how he went about searching for a job, since in the late 40's there were no computers yet, except the huge ones that took up a whole warehouse. Perhaps his old boss at the bottled gas company where he once worked knew someone out west. In any case, after a short time, Daddy had located a job in Phoenix, Arizona, with another bottled gas company, and told us we were moving. Mom went along with the plan, probably hoping, as Daddy surely did, that a change of scenery could mean a fresh start for the family, as well as an improvement to his health.

I was excited at the thought of living in the desert, where we'd see exotic snakes in the wild, not just at the local snake farm, where I loved to pet them and hold them around my neck. My imagination was abuzz with real cowboys, not just my idols in the movies, like Roy Rogers and Gene Autry. I envisioned tall, wide-armed cacti welcoming us along the road, live gila monsters trudging through the hot sand, and orange trees hanging full of fruit in our backyard.

Daddy informed us that we would be driving cross-country and could only take what would fit into the car. Everything else had to be given away or trashed. Since our apartment had come furnished, we didn't have to deal with that part. But my mother was worried about getting rid of the belongings she had painstakingly collected over the years, like pictures, vases, doilies and cookware. She insisted on keeping certain treasures, like her set of real silverware, still in its velvet-lined box, just as she had gotten it from her mother, even though we hardly ever used it except on special holidays. I'm glad she kept it, because I have been enjoying it for many years now. Terry and I were allowed to take only one or two favorite possessions. It was so hard choosing one doll among the many I had. I cried and felt guilty leaving the rest behind, like a bad mother abandoning her children.

As a nine-year-old looking forward to a big adventure, I didn't appreciate the courage my parents must have had to uproot the family and strike out for the unknown. Like pioneers, they must have thought a new place would bring them a better life. I didn't hear my mother complain or try to change Daddy's mind. She often deferred to him in making decisions, anyway, and must have thought he knew what he was doing and trusted that things would work out. Maybe she hoped that their marriage would improve if Daddy were healthier, or maybe she was secretly wishing for some excitement in her life. In any case, she went about getting everything ready, as if this move was the most natural next step in our lives.

When the car was full to the brim, cramping all four of us, Daddy pointed our car westward and off we went. At first, it was fun to watch the scenery change and call out state lines as we crossed them. There used to be big billboard signs announcing each state and depicting something special about the region. But soon, the long, boring days in the car took their toll, even as we tried to stay optimistic. Because we had little money, my parents drove through several nights, alternating at the wheel, and stopping only for gas and quick meals. Unable to stretch our legs on the back seat, Terry and I slept fitfully and woke up cranky.

Sometimes, we paused to briefly admire something special, like the first cotton field we came to in Georgia. Daddy pulled over so we could walk up to a real cotton plant and touch it.

Most of our clothes were made of cotton back then, before the synthetic materials became popular. I was surprised to see that the boll was full of seeds, but soft, nonetheless. When no one was looking, I plucked one and stuck it into my pocket as a souvenir.

Next, we looked forward to crossing the Mississippi River, which I had heard so much about in school. I could sing all the words to "Ol' Man River" by heart and was expecting something spectacular. What a disappointment to see its murky brown waters and disorganized sprawling. It didn't look majestic at all. Where were the paddle wheel boats like those pictured on the front of Mark Twain's books?

As we drove farther west, I was excited at first to see the big, black rigs of the oil wells, but was shocked at the unexpected stench. All of us groaned and held our noses as we passed them.

After a few days on the road, Terry developed a nasty boil on the front of her leg, which she stretched across the back seat to relieve the pain, thereby encroaching on the little space I had. Even though I tried to stay clear of her leg, I kept hitting it accidently, making her cry out in pain. After finally finding a doctor somewhere off the highway to lance the boil, she still had to keep it elevated while it healed, making for an uncomfortable ride for both of us. Finally, to give everyone a much-needed break, our parents decided to use some of their meager funds to pay for a motel for a night.

I still remember the luxuriously warm water of the shower washing away the travel dust, at least temporarily, and the tasty hot meal in the restaurant, our first in days, followed by a glorious night's sleep in a large, comfortable bed, in which I could finally stretch my legs all the way out. The next day, we felt fortified enough to continue our journey. Finally, at the end of the sixth day after leaving Frederick, we arrived in Phoenix.

My early memories of Phoenix were a mix of amazed gawking and active exploration. After spending the first nine years of my life on the east coast with its mass of green trees and grass, I found the sandy soil, scrubby vegetation, towering cacti and barren mountains fascinating. It was a wondrous place for an outdoor-loving, adventurous kid like me. The sunny, dry weather kept me outside playing most of the time, which is what parents expected their kids to do. If one of my parents caught me lingering indoors with a coloring book or paper dolls on a nice day, they'd say, "Patsy, go outside and play."

In jeans and a tee shirt, I'd climb the orange trees in the grove behind our apartment building, occasionally plucking the juicy fruit to eat, or discover secret tunnels in the high brush that led to the living quarters for cowboys or Indians, depending on my mood. Sometimes I'd be Tarzan's wife, cooking a pot of weeds in our hut made of brush and sticks. Other days, I was a cowgirl riding her range of cotton fields next to our parking lot. Electronic games and smart phones hadn't been invented yet. I didn't mind playing by myself, if no other kids were around. In fact, I preferred letting my fantasies run free.

It rarely occurred to me to ask one of my parents to play with me, except on the odd occasion when we needed another player for a board game like Parcheesi, perhaps; then Mom might play if she had finished all of her housework. For the most part, though, parents wanted some peace and quiet without kids around all the time. Also, back then, people were not so afraid of their kids being snatched or molested. Either it was an uncommon event, or the media was not as effective at publicizing it when it happened. Of course, our parents taught us to avoid talking to strangers, refuse gifts from them and stay away from their vehicles.

The neighbor boy, Barry, who lived across the driveway from us, would probably meet today's description of a nerd, but I loved playing with him. He collected bugs of all kinds, keeping some live and some pickled in formaldehyde. I was drawn to his scary scorpions. I would stare at them up close with my nose pressed against the glass jar, while they recoiled and aimed their venomous tails at my face. They must have thought I was some menacing monster ready to pounce on them. My friend also had a pet tarantula that crawled up his arm and perched on his shoulder, eyeing me from a safe distance. While his hairy black legs looked threatening, they moved remarkably gracefully, as if on tiptoe. The spider would jerk backwards at sudden motions towards him, belying his fierce appearance. I declined offers to hold him myself.

One day, there was big excitement in our street when our neighbors showed everyone the horse they'd just bought. He was tall and sleek with a handsome mane and big brown eyes. I had never ridden a horse before, but was immediately enthralled with him, as many a pre-adolescent girl would have been, and asked if I could ride him. I must have imagined an idyllic scene from one of my favorite books, *Black Beauty*, when the young girl rides her majestic horse across a lovely meadow. The owners may have thought I knew how to ride, although they didn't ask. My parents most likely assumed the owners knew the horse and would see to my safety. All of these misguided assumptions colluded to cause the subsequent disaster.

No sooner had I mounted the horse and taken the reins, when he neighed loudly in protest and reared himself up full length onto his hind hooves and threw me off his back onto the ground. It happened so fast that everyone was stunned. Fortunately, I was not injured from the fall, but was almost killed in the next moments when the horse thundered down, stamping his feet near my head several times as if trying to smash me. Luckily, I was able to roll away from him, out of harm's way. As the adults helped me up and tried to console me, the horse took off galloping across the fields, his mane and the reins flying freely behind him.

With heart pounding and hands shaking, I stared wildly after the horse, as if in a trance. Bewildered and speechless, I shook my head in disbelief as the horse disappeared in the distance. What had just happened? Had I done something to upset him? Even though my parents assured me that wasn't the case, I still blamed myself. Someone put their arm around me, but I only felt numbness. My disappointment was staggering.

We later heard that it took the owners, the police and a number of other people many hours to catch the horse and calm him down. It turned out that the owners knew very little about their new acquisition, which they had bought for a bargain price at an auction, and hoped to train. Of course, they had no business letting me get on that horse with no riding experience, especially when they didn't know the horse well.

Although not physically injured, I carried invisible scars from that traumatic incident. It took me years to overcome my fear of horses enough to try to ride again. I made a few half-hearted attempts in college with my roommate Judy to ride near her parents' house in Catonsville, Maryland. We'd rent some tame horses and ride on mostly level trails, usually with a guide in front, but I could never really relax in the saddle, and eventually gave it up. Later in life, I collected brightly painted toy horses made of wood or metal with their hooves secured on wheels or mounted on runners like rocking horses. With their legs kept firmly in place, I could admire the horses for the beautiful creatures they are, without being reminded of that angry runaway beast.

The recommendation by my father's doctor that we move to a drier climate to ease his asthma was indeed a wise one. In Phoenix, he felt much better physically and seemed to be in much better spirits. Best of all, my parents argued much less, making us all happier. But a different kind of problem was now causing them stress: they could hardly make ends meet in Phoenix, where the cost of living was considerably higher than in Maryland where we had lived before.

My father's job with a bottled gas company barely paid enough to cover the bills, so my parents had to scrape to get by. I knew they were worried, but I wasn't directly affected. Tomgirl that I was, I was perfectly content in sneakers and jeans, playing outdoors most of the time that I wasn't in school.

I don't know why my mother didn't get a job – at nine and thirteen my sister and I were certainly old enough to be left alone after school until one of our parents got home.

Mom didn't have any formal training after high school, but could certainly have worked as a waitress or a store clerk somewhere. Maybe transportation was difficult, living as we did on the outskirts of Phoenix with only one car. Also, in 1949 and 1950 when we lived there, it was uncommon for women to work outside of the home. Maybe my mother had never had a job before, and lacked confidence in herself. She had not yet acquired the secretarial skills that would make her an excellent secretary later on when I was older.

To be honest, I wondered what she did all day until I got home from school. The apartment was small and easy to keep clean with two bedrooms, a living room, and a cramped, eat-in kitchen. I remember the time when we had only one can of beans and some crackers left in the cupboard a few days before my father's next payday. This dire situation happened only once, but probably scared my parents into making plans to return east, as soon as my father could find another job.

Whenever my father got a new job or my parents separated, a move meant a change of schools for me and this time was no different. In Phoenix I attended fourth grade in a modern school arranged in an open design of one-story squares around landscaped courtyards with paths connecting the airy classrooms. The buildings were inviting, but I entered each new school with trepidation, hoping the teacher was nice and the kids would like me. I was always the new kid, the one everyone stared at, especially because I often started sometime in the middle of the school year when everyone else had already settled in. One way I tried to fit in was to learn what game was popular in my new class. I tried my best to play well at the new game, in order to be accepted by my classmates. In Frederick it was hopscotch; in Middletown, jump rope; in Milwaukee, jacks; in Norfolk, pick-up-sticks; in Phoenix, marbles. Luckily, I was fairly agile and caught on fast.

During recess, my classmates and I would go outside with our bag of colorful little orbs and draw our circles in the sand. The goal was to knock the opponent's marble out of the circle with my "knocker", thereby winning his marble. I got so good at the game that I usually walked away with a bulging bag. I kept my marbles for ages after we moved back east, where no one I knew played the game. I have no idea what happened to them, but they probably went the way of the yo-yos and trading cards, down a forgotten shaft of discarded treasures.

One day, I was taking a short cut through the cotton field between our house and school when a girl about a year older than I popped up out of nowhere, looking mean. She planted herself in front of me, arms on hips to block my path, and said, "You can't walk through this field. It belongs to my uncle." Without thinking, and surprising myself as I matched her aggressive tone, I replied, "It's a free country and I can walk anywhere I want." When she shouted back that I was trespassing and demanded I get off the field immediately, I said, "You can't tell me what to do. I'll walk through here if I feel like it." One thing led to another until we were engaged in a pushing, shoving, hair pulling, shoulder wrangling, screaming match that took us to the ground and left us full of dirt and not a little blood. I'm not sure how the fight ended – probably in a draw - with both of us running home.

The next thing I remember was stumbling into our apartment, heart racing, with tears and blood dripping down my face – I only had a bloody nose and some scratches on my cheeks, but my mother was horrified. "Patsy, what in the world happened to you?" she screamed. She was not only worried about my injuries, which turned out to be minimal, but also my behavior, as I was not one to get into fights. Once I caught my breath and was able to talk without my voice catching, I explained what had happened. She seemed to understand and didn't chastise me, although I'm sure she wished I had found some other, more peaceful means to handle the dispute. She proceeded to dress my wounds with Mercurochrome and Band-Aids, and then suggested I lie down to calm my nerves.

When my father came home that evening and heard about the incident, he applauded me for standing up for myself and said the girl had it coming to her. He almost always took my side when I had problems with people. He'd assume that I used good judgment and acted appropriately, which wasn't necessarily always the case. He sometimes overlooked my responsibility in the interaction, automatically blaming the other party. But I knew I could count on his support. He was one of my biggest cheerleaders in life, and encouraged me many times to take difficult stands on matters of principle. I don't remember for certain whether I walked through that cotton field again, but if I did, I'm sure I scanned the area carefully first.

Through the many windows of our fourth grade classroom, we could see the most striking landmark of the town, Camelback Mountain, a low-slung range of hills in the shape of a camel resting on his belly with his knees folded underneath him, his head held high and his hump clearly visible. It was devoid of any trees, consisting mostly of boulders, sagebrush and cacti in every size. We used to have cookouts there and watch the sun set. The colorful sky would set the mountain ablaze in wild reds and bright golds, then slowly turn to dark purple, silhouetting the camel in black. Once, while running along a desert path, I tripped and fell into a cactus, puncturing my hands with countless thorns, some of which stayed painfully imbedded for many weeks. Armed with tweezers, my mother would hover over my hands while I flinched at each extraction. Surprisingly, we never encountered any snakes on our outings, nor did spiders or scorpions ever bite us.

My mother made friends with a woman named Pat, who lived a few doors down from us. We called her "Big Pat" to avoid confusing her with me, since I was called Patsy. She was big in a number of ways, not fat, but voluminous of body and personality. She wore colorful clothing with trailing scarves and laughed loudly, showing a mouthful of beautiful, white teeth. She had an open, generous spirit. She seemed to embody some of the characteristics that I think my mother secretly envied, especially her outgoingness. They sat for hours drinking coffee and smoking cigarettes during the day. Big Pat and her husband owned the first television in the neighborhood. It was tiny, a scant twelve inches, very hard to see, especially with a bunch of us crowded around it, trying to catch a glimpse. The picture was often fuzzy, or jumped up and down, or had squiggly lines going across it, while the sound was almost unintelligible. Still, we loved it. It was a magical invention, mesmerizing for kids and adults, and Big Pat loved playing hostess. She'd greet us at the door with a smile and offer to make everyone drinks, usually Kool-Aid, and popcorn.

Big Pat hated housework. She would let the dust bunnies build up for weeks to the point where even she couldn't stand it anymore, then moan and groan for days about how she needed to clean house. My mother was a meticulous housekeeper and must have mentioned to her friend that I was a good helper at our house. The next thing I knew, Big Pat was offering to pay me to clean her house. I was ten by now and, this being my first job, didn't know what to charge. She said she would save up my "salary" and when it reached a certain amount, she would take me wherever I wanted for a fancy lunch. I had overheard the adults talking about a place in Phoenix called "The Golden Flame", which I was dying to visit. It was famous not only for its food, but for its jungle-like atmosphere. There were live parrots flying around the dining room, and some monkeys in cages between the tables, all set among lush tropical flora. It was the "in" place and I couldn't wait to see it.

For many weeks, I worked for Big Pat to save up enough money and, finally, the big day came: we were going to "The Golden Flame" for lunch. Big Pat got all decked out, fancier than usual, and I wore my best polka-dotted dress. In her shiny sedan, she drove me downtown, where she had the valet park the car. Even in the daylight the neon sign of the restaurant was brightly blazing its flames of gold. My heart jumped with excitement as the maitre d' led us to our reserved table. I had never experienced such luxury before. My eyes drank in the posh surroundings, the linen tablecloths, fresh flowers, velour-covered chairs, and the bowing waiter, amid the squawking cacophony of brightly feathered birds flitting above and around us. I have no recollection of what we ate, but I remember being served a large, iced Coca-Cola in a tall, frosty glass with a miniature, Japanese umbrella on top. I felt very special.

One day, Big Pat announced that she and her family had to leave town. Something had apparently gone wrong with her husband's job. It happened so fast that I've always wondered if something shady was going on. Still, we were sorry to see them go, and take their "joie de vivre" with them, not to mention their television set and my cleaning job. The neighborhood was never the same after they left.

Meanwhile, Daddy continued looking for better jobs. In his search he found an opportunity with Esso Standard Oil Company too good to ignore, even though it meant moving back east. The stipulation was that if he passed a six-week training class, he could become a manager of a truck stop in Thurmont, Maryland.

We were thrilled for him the day he got the news that he had been accepted into the program. He seemed both proud and worried about going back to school after so many years and he didn't want to leave us to take the course back east. But he did well, passed his exam, and earned his operator's license. Next, he leased the business in Thurmont, which consisted of a large gas station and diner, both open 24 hours a day. Thus, at the age of 40, Daddy became the manager of his own business.

What might have been daunting for some people, Daddy seemed to take in stride. He had always told my sister and me that we could do anything we set our minds to, and must have believed that of himself, as well. At the time, it seemed like just another job Daddy was starting, but I realize now what a risk he was taking. To my knowledge, he had had absolutely no experience in running a garage and had never so much as worked in a restaurant before. But he was determined to better our finances, and thrilled to be his own boss at last. His motto was that if you really wanted something and were willing to work hard for it, you could succeed.

I always thought I would one day go back to Phoenix, but I never did. If asked to name five U.S. cities where I might want to live, it would certainly be among them, at least the way I remember it from 1950. I'd like to see if Camelback Mountain is still as impressive to my adult eyes as it was when I was ten. I might re-visit the state park and watch the sunsets. I might go down the road from our apartment complex and see if the public pool is still there, the one in which I swam countless laps one summer under my father's tutelage, increasing the number of laps each visit until I could swim a whole mile. It was an exhilarating accomplishment, but exhausting, and, quite honestly, a bit boring at the end. Still, I was glad I did it and I felt proud of myself. Last but not least, I would go downtown and look for "The Golden Flame", although it's probably long gone. However, if I should find it, I would order an ice-cold Coca-Cola again and ask for a tiny Japanese umbrella to go with it.

Esther Williams

*   *   *

ESTHER WILLIAMS, THE POPULAR MOVIE actress of the 40's and 50's who specialized in water ballet, was one of my biggest childhood idols. I must have "discovered" her when I was ten or eleven years old and was mesmerized by her grace and charm, both as an actress and as a swimmer, especially when she swam under water. I saw all of Esther's movies, some of them multiple times. I wanted to be like her, to swim beautifully and effortlessly, and be admired, as she was, by handsome men, who pursued her in the love stories she played.

Esther's feathery strokes left no ripples, as if she were gliding through air, and her lovely smile endured, whether she swam on top of, or underneath, the water. She had a gorgeous figure, the likes of which I hoped I would grow into one day. When I first started watching her movies, I hadn't even begun to develop a bosom, but I wore my two-piece, red bathing suit, imagining myself in her place just the same. I dreamed of being a beautiful swimming star like Esther, and practiced every chance I got.

Luckily, everyone in my family liked swimming, which was one of the few activities we shared. My parents, my sister, and I enjoyed spending the day at the pool or the lake, where I could often be found slithering elegantly under water, trying to do the breast stroke like Esther did, while trying to maintain a smile without choking. Sometimes when swimming on top of the water, I would concentrate on arching my arms just like she did, looking straight ahead into an invisible camera, while trying to breathe without grimacing. I kept my fingers together, so as not to make a splash when I did the crawl stroke. Swimming backwards was a challenge, because I wanted to maintain the same easy rhythm, yet not run into anything. I didn't have a film director to warn me, as I'm sure Esther did.

I used to time myself with a stopwatch at the pool or in the bathtub to see how long I could stay under water. After much practice I eventually worked up to over a minute before running out of breath. In her movies Esther spent seemingly endless amounts of time submerged, doing wonderfully artistic scenes, like a mermaid who needed no air. One of her best acts included doing a slow backward summersault in the water, leaving one leg pointed straight up in the air out of the water, then letting it gradually disappear straight down under the surface. Even her big toe didn't move the water. As much as I tried to master this maneuver, I often ended up with a nose full of water and feeling klutzy. Then, after much effort, I was finally able to do a halfway decent imitation.

There weren't any opportunities for me to participate in water ballet, since there were no classes near our house. Had we lived in California, I probably would have joined a water ballet troupe and may have ended up with a very different career. For a while, I continued to rehearse alone, but my fervor was waning without a proper teacher. However, I still wanted to keep swimming any chance I got.

One day, as a young teenager, I noticed an ad announcing a class in Junior Lifesaving to be taught by the Red Cross at the local YMCA in Waynesboro, Pennsylvania. I worried about whether I could pass the qualifying test, which involved swimming a certain number of lengths of the pool, treading water for a proscribed length of time and holding my breath under water. I think Esther's spirit was with me as I accomplished each task with flying colors, and went on to complete the class and earn the first of several swimming badges.

At sixteen I became a Senior Lifesaver, which landed me a part-time job one summer at the local public pool in Hagerstown, Maryland, teaching swimming to children and adults. I was thrilled to share my aquatic skills and experience with my students and found it gratifying to watch them develop their own sense of confidence and competence from one lesson to the next. I also thought it was important that people know how to swim for their own safety, and I felt good about teaching as a community service, since the pay was very low. I hadn't completely lost interest in water ballet, but my enthusiasm was definitely shifting. If I couldn't be a swimming performer, I could at least be a swimming instructor.

At seventeen I went to an aquatics camp for a week to earn a certificate as a Water Safety Instructor. This class included learning how to teach diving, canoeing, and general safety on and in the water. To practice life saving, they had us put on clothes over our swim suits, including jeans, a long sleeve shirt and sneakers, then jump into deep water and take them all off while not losing sight of the "victim" we were supposed to save. If getting the shirt and sneakers off was tedious while treading water constantly, removing the jeans almost did me in. I find jeans hard enough to put on and take off when they are dry, much less sopping wet. At the end, I was huffing and puffing. Next, we had to approach the victim, who was pretending to struggle, and tow him under our arm to safety, which was about 25 yards. By the time I deposited my "victim" on the shore of the lake, I was exhausted.

The instructors had made it look so easy. They were muscular athletes who had built up stamina from doing these rescue maneuvers for years. I vowed then and there never to try to save someone unless they were in a swimming pool and within easy reach of the side. Even then, I'd keep my distance, using a bamboo pole or a buoy; otherwise, a double drowning, which they taught us to avoid, would be a definite possibility.

The summer after graduating high school I was hired to be one of the swimming and water safety instructors at an exclusive girls' camp near Blue Ridge Summit, Pennsylvania. It was situated on beautiful, rolling acres in the lower Blue Ridge Mountains, with cabins, tennis courts, various activities' buildings, a dining hall, infirmary, a lake and an Olympic-size, outdoor swimming pool. The swimming program had a colored-coded system of swim caps to differentiate among various levels of the swimmers' competency, with beginners wearing yellow caps, intermediate, red caps, advanced, blue caps and most proficient, white caps. Most of the campers came year after year and tried to advance one color each season. The white caps were truly magnificent swimmers, strong and graceful, who glided through the water with hardly a splash, just like Esther Williams.

The highlight of each summer was a water ballet performed by the campers for their parents when they visited on parents' weekend. All the water safety staff was involved in some way in getting the production ready. I assisted with choreographing the show, even though I had never done anything like it before. Some of the "old timers", camp counselors who had worked there many summers and had seen a number of ballets, gave me some ideas, but my best inspiration came from my memories of Esther's movie ballets. Armed with a giant roll of brown paper and a fistful of magic markers, I worked with the other water instructors to compose various water formations, drawing in swimmers' heads, arms and legs for points of stars and centers of blossoms. The tricky part was finding a role in the water show for each swimmer's level, so that she looked her best and felt good about her performance. We spent days choosing songs to best fit the routines we created, until, finally, it all started to come together.

When the big day arrived, the parking lot filled up with long, low Lincolns and Cadillacs, full of parents anxious to see their kids again after two weeks of camp, and admire their accomplishments. They wended their way down the hill to the pool, where bleachers had been set up for them. The butterflies in my stomach were flying overtime, as the overture of the ballet resounded over the loud speakers, first with a scratchy squawk, then settling into a smooth sound wafting across the pool. The water ballet had begun.

I watched in wonder as the girls sailed through the patterns they had practiced so diligently. They did such an admirable job, I could have kissed each of their wet caps as they emerged from the water after the finale. Their broad smiles showed that they were proud of themselves, too. Their parents' applause reverberated across the hills, echoing their appreciation of the show, while I breathed a sigh of relief. Even though the ballet was a big success, it had been a nerve-wracking experience for me, one I did not care to repeat. Delving into the nitty-gritty mechanics of graceful ballet swimming: the timing, the breathing, the muscle control – plus the stage jitters before the show - had taken away some of the magic. I hadn't known what hard work it took to put on a water show. But it didn't dampen my spirits for swimming. It has remained one of my favorite activities, both for exercise and pleasure, throughout my life.

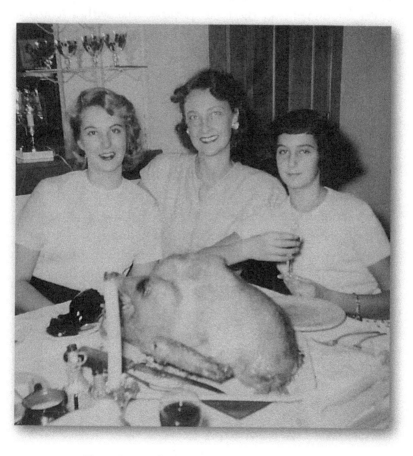

Terry, Iris and Patsy Overstreet, circa 1952

fault for taunting him. Mostly though, he was good-natured and we loved him.

Mom called Tarfeathers "persnickety" because he insisted on eating our leftovers, never store bought dog food. She would carefully cut up pieces of meat, potatoes and vegetables in bite-size portions for him, and worry over him while he ate. He would sometimes come with me on my forays into the woods, but he'd later complain when I tried to remove the burrs that got into his long hair.

Our house was situated on park-like grounds called Locust Grove, which consisted of an inn and several cottages, along with a few rental houses, all owned by an imposing lady of wide girth, Nora Hoffmaster, who spoke with a German accent and reeked of raw garlic, which she chewed to ward off colds. I remember thinking I'd rather get the colds than smell like her. She was a generous soul at heart, allowing her granddaughter Judy and me to romp around the unoccupied rooms of her inn, or - this was our favorite - spend the night in one of the empty cottages. We'd overlook the cottage's cobwebs and musty odor from being closed up and pretend we were grand ladies, vacationing in one of our many resorts without a care in the world. We'd munch on popcorn and drink ginger ale, special treats allowed us for the evening.

But sometimes, late at night, a knock-knocking at the window made us clutch the covers and sink down into the safety of the pillows. Then the noise would stop and we'd laugh nervously, explaining aloud to each other and ourselves that it had just been a branch scratching at the windowpane. At all costs, we had to prove that we were brave and could stick it out. Nowadays, most parents wouldn't think of letting two young girls stay alone in a cottage, but parents were more trusting back then, and they were only about 50 yards away from us.

There wasn't much to the sleepy little village of Blue Ridge, its shortened name, perched as it was on top of a mountain, but it was perfect as my stomping grounds. Since the area was considered safe in those days, I was free to wander around at will. Crime was practically unheard of there. The only rules were to be home by suppertime, wash and dry the dishes with my sister and do my homework, all of which I did willingly. I never rebelled against my parents. Since we didn't have a trash pick-up service, I was also entrusted to burn the trash in a rusty old drum used for that purpose up the hill from the house. I loved staring into the flames, but took care that the sparks didn't do any mischief. I think my father hauled the garbage down to the truck stop for disposal.

Blue Ridge had been popular as a summer resort before the days of air-conditioning. People used to come from Baltimore and Washington to stay at one of the hotels and catch the mountain breezes. It had even had its own railway station, now standing vacant, but still kept groomed in the old style with fresh green and gold paint and adorned with colorful flower boxes and a miniature, black locomotive. A tiny strip mall across the street had a drug store, post office, bank and a combination hardware/dime store, certainly all anybody could want for their daily needs. When I had a little pocket money – I didn't get regular allowance – I'd walk up to the drug store and buy one of my favorite comic books, either "Little Lulu" or "Archie," or buy a delicious, Breyer's vanilla ice cream cone. If I went there with Daddy, he'd sometimes spring for the best soda fountain treat in the world, a hot fudge sundae peaked with whipped cream and a bright red cherry.

Catty-cornered from the bank was a large, grey stone building, which housed the Episcopal Church, the town hall and, tucked away on the second floor, a small library. Being curious, one day I ventured up the stairs by myself to find out how to borrow books. The nice librarian eased my shyness and explained how it worked. Thus began my lifelong love affair with reading and learning. I always forgot to bring the books back on time, though, and had to pay the going fines back then of two cents per book per day. No one at home ever reminded me of the due dates. To my knowledge, I was the only one in my family that used a library at that time. To this day, I still can't seem to return books on time.

One day, in the church hallway that led to the library, I saw a notice for piano lessons. Since our house came furnished with a piano in the dining room, I had wanted to learn how to play it. I had learned a bit from the funeral parlor neighbor, but had never had a professional teacher. I was thrilled when my parents agreed to let me start lessons. I think my mother met the teacher once, but mostly I went to the lessons by myself and organized my practice times myself. I was used to doing things on my own.

My piano teacher was a burly, energetic man with white hair, who seemed to take up the whole piano bench when he demonstrated a new piece to me. He liked to laugh and made my lessons fun. Transforming the written notes onto the ivory keys to produce music was like magic, prompting me to practice enthusiastically every day after school. Sadly, however, my lessons came to an abrupt halt after only a few, short months.

During one lesson, as my teacher stood next to me while I played my pieces for him, I noticed an odor of alcohol on his breath. I recognized the smell from my parents who drank "highballs" when friends came over for bridge parties. I never thought much of it, but when he was suddenly let go with no explanation, I thought it might be because of his drinking. I've always wondered what happened to him and hope he found a place where he could live happily as his exuberant self. Unfortunately, they never found another piano teacher to replace him, at least not while we lived there. Thus ended my brief encounter with piano lessons, which were not to resume until many years later in Germany after I was married.

On one of my jaunts, I discovered the Opportunity Shop, a thrift shop down the street from the strip mall, run by the church ladies for charity. I loved milling around, looking for affordable treasures to hide away and later put under the Christmas tree for the family: a painted plate for Mom, an ash tray for Daddy, a hand mirror for Terry, all for a dollar or two each. I still enjoy searching for good bargains at consignment shops, especially near upper class neighborhoods where the findings can be startling. It's amazing what nice things people discard. Although I didn't know it at the time, my parents were rather frugal. They taught us to appreciate and take care of what we had. We bought new things only on special occasions, like birthdays and Christmas. We paid into a savings account at the bank regularly, and gave to charity within our means. Even later when I no longer had to count pennies, I still valued thriftiness and ingenuity.

During my wanderings around the village of Blue Ridge, I saw a poster advertising the start-up of a new Girl Scout troop, describing activities, like weaving, knitting, and building bonfires, all of which interested me. My parents had no objection, so off I went to the weekly meetings doing crafts, and on weekends hiking and overnight camping. Here, too, I went on my own. My mother rarely went with me – I don't think she even knew my troop leader's name - but she'd always send a batch of her crispy Toll House cookies for parties at my activities, including school, when parent participation was requested.

The Girl Scout manual was chock full of descriptions and directions how to earn merit badges on a variety of topics, ranging from potting plants to identifying constellations, enough to keep me happily busy. Before long, a slew of merit badges paraded down the sash across my chest. I felt especially proud when my mother came to one of the awards ceremonies. Achieving honors inside and outside school became more and more important to me, as if I defined myself by how well I did. I craved the attention and recognition, perhaps too much.

Still, discovering so many personal opportunities came at just the right time in my development during the four years we lived in Blue Ridge Summit. The village formed an idyllic backdrop for me, a young, inquisitive girl who loved freedom and the outdoors. I was lucky to have that time growing up in a wholesome community where I learned hobbies and skills that would satisfy and sustain me later on.

But sometimes I wonder if I had too much freedom. On the one hand, I was becoming self-reliant, but on the other hand, I may not have been getting sufficient interest and involvement from my parents. They weren't disinterested, but didn't take initiative to make sure that I was all right and that I was connected to people who promoted my well being. I know they had their own problems, but if they had been able to participate more in my activities, I could have carried the image of their faces with me, and felt more secure.

My motivation to discover the world seemed to rest solely on my inner drive. I think I was lonely at times, and didn't realize it. Perhaps if I had asked my parents for more guidance or company, I would have gotten it, but at an unconscious level I may not have wanted to bother them. Mom seemed worried by her troublesome marriage much of the time. When she complained about how badly Daddy treated her, apparently looking for validation, I tried to avoid her. I hated feeling caught in the middle of their problems and didn't want to take sides. Like most kids, I loved both of my parents and didn't want to pit one against the other. Yet, I felt like I was letting her down through my silence. No wonder I had a nervous stomach at times and frequent nightmares. Thank heavens I could escape to the outdoors, walking or riding my bike around Locust Grove to find comfort and peace in the arms of Mother Nature.

Staying busy, working hard and playing sports may have been a way for me to mask my feelings, although I didn't realize it at the time, and to get positive attention, especially from my father. He rarely asked me how I felt about anything, just how well I was doing, for example grade-wise at school. He used to give me a quarter for every A I got. Mainly though, I was like a playmate for him, pitching ball, playing ping-pong, throwing horseshoes, playing badminton and diving off the high board, all of which he had taught me.

Aside from sports, I usually took initiative in finding other activities and developing skills in them. My sense of competence was at once a strength, in that it built self-confidence, and a hindrance, in that it kept me from asking for support, giving the impression that I didn't need it. I may have deluded myself into believing that I could take care of my own needs alone, without help from other people. Later in life, this belief would interfere with my relationships.

Sister Mary Incarnata and Patsy, 1954

St. Andrew's Catholic School

＊　＊　＊

ALTHOUGH MY FAMILY WASN'T CATHOLIC, I attended St. Andrew's Catholic School in Waynesboro, Pennsylvania, while we lived in Blue Ridge Summit. It was known to be better than the public schools in the area and my mother believed that nuns were excellent teachers. It was a small school with only four nuns, each of whom taught two grade levels combined into one class. They were all strict, allowing no talking in the halls, tolerating no tardiness, and frowning at gum-chewing, even during recess. They had only to stare at us in silence to get immediate attention and obedience. It was understood that we were there to learn, not to play around.

Our eighth grade teacher, Sister Mary Incarnata was the toughest of the group. She towered above us at about 5' 10" and looked severe in her long black habit and blazing white wimple. She could frighten us by raising a single eyebrow. Her giant wooden rosary beads rattled against each other among the expansive folds of her skirt and would announce her approach to the classroom, causing us to scurry to our seats and sit upright. No one dared push her to see what she'd really do if confronted. None of the nuns used physical discipline; they didn't have to. A few biting words to humiliate or intimidate were powerful enough.

At home I knew when it was Sunday night by my churning stomach – a nervous anticipation of school the next day that had begun in fifth grade when I started going to St. Andrew's. I was afraid that I had forgotten to do part of my homework, or that I had made mistakes on it, or that I would forget the piece we had to memorize for the next day's assignment. I was a good student and usually got honor roll grades, but still felt uneasy. What if I messed up this time? Sister's reaction seemed to have only two modes: glowing praise or harsh disapproval. She didn't waste time in the grey area of partial credit. You came out of class either on top of the world, having named all the countries of Europe in alphabetical order, or feeling like an idiot, having missed one of your times tables. When Sister was in a good mood, her sarcasm was less stinging. She'd lean into you at your desk and bellow: "Well, I hope your mother loves you!" I remember being surprised at her sweet talcum powder smell as she passed by, a scent so unlike her personality.

In all fairness, the nuns sometimes tried to make us feel special in their way. For example, I was chosen numerous times to go over to the convent at lunch time to do the nuns' dishes for them. The job was presented as an honor, one that only a trustworthy, competent person received and I felt proud to be asked. By contrast, at home my sister and I were expected to do the dishes as our responsibility in the household. Protesting fell on deaf ears. Our parents could have learned something from the nuns about manipulating children.

I liked getting an inside view of the nuns' house, which had seemed, until then, a mysterious inner sanctum. From the kitchen I could see a tiny room with kneeling benches that served as a chapel for the nuns, a small, sparsely furnished parlor, and the bottom of a flight of stairs.

One day, when there had been more pots and pans involved in the cooking than usual, Sister told me to finish up, then lock the door myself and come late to the afternoon classes. For the first time, I was alone in the convent. I had always wanted to see where the nuns slept, and this was my opportunity. Even though I believed that upstairs was off limits, my curiosity tempered my anxiety as I walked down the hallway.

With a racing pulse, I tiptoed up the stairs. At the top, I could see four open doors revealing identical, small rooms, each with the same stark white walls and austere furniture: a narrow, iron-frame bed, a plain dresser and one wooden chair without arms. A sad crucifix hung above each of the beds, which were made with white sheets and an unadorned bedspread. The bare hardwood floors were scrubbed and polished to a high sheen and smelled like the oil of my father's garage. As I went back down the stairs, my young mind wondered how a person's spirituality could override all the creature comforts I took for granted. It seemed almost cruel, and I vowed never to consider the nunnery for myself.

Easing back into the classroom, I kept my head down, and hoped that my brazen escapade didn't show in my face. We believed that the nuns had extrasensory powers, that they could see through us, could read our minds, and know when we were lying. We also thought that nuns were perfect, and couldn't imagine what they would tell the priest during confession. I was shocked when Sister told me a lie one day in the playground.

I had walked to the photo shop during lunchtime to pick up pictures that my classmate, Fred, and I had taken of each other in various flirty poses, including some of us kissing. When Sister saw me coming with the photo package in my hand, she immediately grabbed it and said, "Oh, Patsy, let me see your pictures." My heart sank as I realized I couldn't escape, and my breath almost stopped as she fingered through the photos, her jaw dropping farther at each scene. She and I were both horrified and momentarily speechless, each for a different reason. Finally she exclaimed, "Why, Patsy, these pictures are shameful. I'm so disappointed in you. I thought you were a nice girl. You know, even actors in the movies don't do these things in real life. They use trick photography to make it look like they embrace."

I don't remember what else she said, because my brain lurched back into gear when she claimed that actors don't really kiss on the screen. I knew this wasn't true and felt confused at first, then angry that she would think me so naïve. Maybe she couldn't handle the truth of my sexual awakening and wanted me to stay a little girl in her eyes. But at age thirteen I already knew a thing or two, and I knew for sure that I wanted more kisses. Yet, I was left with a vague apprehension that what Fred and I did was wrong. I had always thought of nuns as having unquestionable moral authority. Sister threatened to tell my parents about the photos, but she never did. I worried for weeks that they would be angry with me, too. They didn't know about my new interest in kissing boys and I wasn't sure how they'd feel about it.

I'll never know why Sister made up that story about actors not really kissing. I wondered whether she had ever had a boyfriend and been kissed. It seemed unfair and unnatural to me that nuns were expected to live without physical love. I certainly didn't want to do that. Why couldn't they live a religious life and enjoy physical affection as well? I resented the implication that I was somehow impure for wanting real kisses in my life.

Once, I argued with Sister about the need for martyrs to die for their beliefs. It didn't make sense to me and seemed like such a waste. We had been studying the lives of various saints and how they were put to death for being Christian, some in the most horrible ways, usually involving torture, like burning at the stake or being ripped apart by lions. Why couldn't they have just pretended not to be Christians, I reasoned. If they had simply denied their faith in order to save themselves, perhaps they could have found secret ways to spread the word of God. What good were they to anyone when dead? Since God was all-knowing, He would know that, in their hearts, they still believed in Him. Besides, I asked, why would a kind, benevolent God want His worshippers to suffer like that? Sister's jaw dropped momentarily as she stared at me and gathered her arguments. Taking a deep breath, she straightened her spine and began her patient explanation.

Basically, she said that the martyrs had to tell the truth, not deny their God and had to show that they would endure anything to confirm their allegiance to Him. Their suffering would impress the heathens to understand how strong the Christian faith was, and confirm their belief in the afterlife. In dying for Christ, as He had died for us on the cross, they were assured a place in heaven. Sister exhaled deeply, sounding satisfied with her answer, but I wasn't convinced. I also realized that, in her book, some lies were more acceptable than others.

The nuns had pat answers for any questions regarding Catholicism. There was neither grey area, nor room for discussion. For religion class we students had to memorize the questions and answers as outlined in the catechism. For example, there were exact descriptions of, and penalties for, venial (minor) and mortal (major) sins, which had to be confessed to the priest. Venial sins were small transgressions like spreading gossip or stealing an apple. Mortal sins were serious crimes like adultery or murder. The priest would then dole out the penance needed to erase the sin from the person's soul, like saying ten "Hail Marys," or praying the rosary three times in the case of venial sins.

As a non-Catholic, I wasn't allowed to go to confession, but I had to "examine my conscience" just like the rest of the class. This exercise made me focus on what I'd done wrong, making me feel guilty. On the one hand, it was consoling for me to learn that sins, if properly atoned for, didn't count against you. You could wipe the slate clean, so to speak, and start fresh, trying to be good. On the other hand, it was scary for me to learn that if you died with a venial sin unconfessed, you'd go to purgatory, a fiery, but temporary place, where you could be punished for your sins and still go to heaven. But with a mortal sin on your soul, you had no chance and would go straight to hell for all eternity.

Although the definitive structure of these rules was reassuring in a way, the thought of making an irrevocable mistake caused me much trepidation. Still, I found the rites and rituals so appealing that, after a couple of years at St. Andrew's, I asked my parents if I could join the church. Of course, the nuns had hoped all along that I would convert. My parents were aghast at the very suggestion and said absolutely not. Strange, that they allowed me to be educated by the nuns in all areas, but neglected to realize the strong spiritual influence that would have on me. I was disappointed in my parents' reaction, which I didn't really understand, but trusted that they had good reasons for it.

When I was about halfway through the eighth grade, my parents decided to separate again, and began to unravel our household at Locust Grove. My father was renting a room at a motel; my sister, now almost 18, was moving in with a girlfriend; and my mother was going to her mother's until she figured out what to do. In the meantime, I wanted to graduate with my class in Waynesboro. With the help of the nuns, arrangements were made for me to stay with a Catholic family, the Shrivers, who were members at St. Andrew's, so my school year would not be disrupted. I was thankful, but apprehensive about living with strangers, and worried about my parents and sister. I also felt angry and embarrassed, as if my family had abandoned me, and I was now an orphan.

Fortunately, Sophie and Bill did all they could to put me at ease. A devout and generous couple, they agreed to take me into their home for about six months, until June graduation. I think Daddy paid them something for my stay, but the expectation was that I would help Sophie with the children and housework. She didn't outline specific tasks for me, however, which led to misunderstandings later.

They had fixed up a room for me on the second floor of their house, with freshly washed curtains on the windows and matching bedspread. A crucifix hung above the single bed. They often hugged each other and laughed with their children, two-year old Joseph and infant Mary. Sophie had soft, warm eyes and Bill was one of the handsomest men I'd ever seen. Sophie once confided in me that she was so crazy about Bill when they first met that she promised God if Bill asked her to marry him, she would name her first two children Joseph and Mary in His honor. Theirs was another happy, respectful marriage that I witnessed first hand, in addition to my Aunt Ruby's and Uncle G.C.'s marriage in Roanoke, strengthening my belief that a happy marriage was indeed possible.

Although I had done some baby-sitting for a neighbor in Blue Ridge, I really had little knowledge or experience taking care of small children. To be honest, it was tedious and often boring for me to stay cooped up inside, entertaining a toddler. Joseph was a happy, playful little kid and fairly easy to manage, but after about half an hour reading to him or playing with him, I began to feel trapped and longed to be outside, walking around town, looking for adventure. As a young adolescent, my hormonal juices were bubbling up, demanding attention.

Early on in my stay at their house, Sophie and I had a falling out. One particular Saturday afternoon I had made plans to meet a classmate downtown and maybe go to the movies, without asking Sophie first. As I was about to head out the door, Sophie stopped and asked me where I was going. I told her I was meeting my friend Joyce in town. "But we clean house on Saturdays," she said. "I thought you were going to help me."

I was confused. I thought I had already helped her. "I just did the dishes this morning," I said.

"Well, that's just part of the everyday routine. There's a lot more to do."

"Like what?" I asked.

She went on to describe all the things she expected, like vacuuming, dusting and scrubbing the kitchen floor. When I told her Saturday was the only time I could go out and have fun with my friends, she replied, "Well, it's not fair for you to go out and leave me with the children and all the housework."

Since I had already set up the date with Joyce, Sophie reluctantly let me go that day, but I felt guilty about it. I also thought she was being unreasonable. After all, I was only a visitor, not a member of their family. Later, I understood that Sophie was expecting me to help in all aspects of the housework, like a modern-day au pair, whereas I thought doing a few chores, like I had done at home, was enough and I'd be free the rest of the day. We eventually worked it out, but I wished we had sat down in the beginning and made an exact list of my chores, so I could have done them independently and then be off duty.

I had a crush on one of the boys in my class at school and told Sophie about it. She grinned and said she remembered those days when she was my age. Then I met another cute boy at a dance and swooned to her over him. I seemed to thrive on the attention of several boys at once. One was not enough. When Sophie called me "fickle," my feelings were hurt, even though I wasn't sure what the word meant, but I could tell from her disapproving expression that it wasn't good. Looking back, I can see that this was the start of a tendency of mine to seek the attention and affection of multiple suitors, as if the number of males interested in me determined my self worth. I also wondered if the next man I met might be better than the last, making me hesitate to make a commitment.

As an adult many years later, I visited Sophie, who was still living at the same address. She looked just as beautiful, even with her grey hair. With a smile she told me that she and Bill had ended up having eleven children together, and adding on to the house three times. First, the outside wall of my old room had been broken out to build deeper into the backyard. After more children came, they built upward, making a third floor to accommodate them. She said she loved having a houseful of kids and couldn't have imagined a happier life. She would be forever grateful.

I envied her ability to appreciate the life she had had and to have loved one man completely, never doubting her choice. Her life was like a fairy tale come true - for her. But I couldn't imagine a similar life making me happy. I didn't know yet what kind of life I wanted for myself, but I knew for sure that being a housewife stuck at home raising a gang of kids was not the dream I yearned for.

Ben's Truck Stop
Thurmont, Maryland

The Truck Stop

*   *   *

IN 1951, WHEN MY FATHER leased the truck stop from Esso Standard Oil Company in Thurmont, he set about making it his own. First, he named it "Ben's Truck Stop", after his own first name, Benjamin. Then, he had the name painted in large letters across the top of the entrance of the low, sprawling building. A huge, oval Esso sign mounted atop a sturdy, steel pole announced the station up and down Route 15, long before you could see the place. Daddy walked proudly in his new manager's shirt with "Ben's" stitched across the chest pocket. He had done well with just a high school diploma, and, after working at many other jobs as someone else's employee, he was thrilled to be the boss of his own business.

The front part of the filling station had islands with normal gas pumps to fill passenger cars. Since there was no self service back then, a loud clang from an air hose would sound as a car rolled over it, summoning an attendant to dispense gas, check the oil and water, and clean the windshield, while the driver stayed inside the vehicle. I sometimes provided the easier part of the service, like cleaning the windows and taking the payment inside.

Daddy loved to tell how, on several occasions, President Eisenhower's cavalcade of limousines stopped on the way to Camp David to gas up their vehicles. Because of the tinted windows, he wasn't sure whether the president himself was inside one of them, but he liked to think that he was. I only saw a disappointing, single limousine at the gas tanks a few times, driven by a uniformed chauffeur, who seemed to be alone.

The side area of Ben's held islands with diesel fuel for the big 18-wheelers. It wasn't a huge operation, but sometimes there were as many as six semis parked on the lot. When I was preparing to get my driver's license, my father had me practice driving in reverse all around the trucks until I was confident in my ability. To this day, I can back into any reasonable parking space on the first try. I feel proud when I notice a pedestrian watching me, nodding their head in approval and I think of my father giving me a thumbs-up whenever I got it right.

Inside the front door, sundry items like combs, cigarettes, No-Doze and air fresheners surrounded the cash register. There were also cheap gift items, such as hula girl lamps, sets of toilet water with talcum powder, and embroidered, boxed hankies, to serve as last minute birthday gifts for the wives of truckers with no time to shop in real stores. Once, when my father tried bringing my mother one of these offerings, he was greeted with an offended expression that he never forgot.

Next to my father's office was a bunkroom, where road-weary truck drivers could take a nap and shower, and a storage room with supplies such as stacks of toilet paper for the restrooms and liquid soap for the dispensers. At one end of the building was the garage where mechanics worked on cars, usually changing oil, replacing batteries, or fixing flat tires. My father didn't have the space or the know-how to do extensive vehicle repairs. If someone's car really broke down, he'd tow it to a fully equipped garage in Frederick, half an hour away.

The garage side of Ben's had a distinctive odor, a mixture of gas, grease and metal, the same odor of my father's hands after working a long shift. Try as he may to clean them, his fingers were permanently stained and splotchy from oily motors. It was impossible for him to keep his fingernails clean, much to Mom's dismay.

The business also came with a small diner, which was at the other end of the building. Although my father had no restaurant experience, not even as a waiter, he dove right in, as he often did with new ventures, figuring, "how hard can it be?" It turned out to be very hard to run two new businesses at once, but he trusted himself to learn the ropes and be successful, sometimes working 15-hour days. Ironically, the hardest part was not handling the auto maintenance and repair, or the administrative procedures of running the station, or planning the menu and ordering food for the kitchen, but finding reliable staff to work the three shifts on both sides of the truck stop, which was open 24 hours a day. Daddy was often short-handed. Some employees would call in sick at the last minute, or not show up at all, which meant that he had to hustle to find help or work extra shifts himself. The small town of Thurmont didn't offer a large pool of potential employees to choose from. Sometimes my mother would pitch in and work in the diner, but she complained about the long hours of standing on her feet.

I, on the other hand, was thrilled anytime I got to help out, which was fairly frequently, from around age thirteen to seventeen. The truck stop was like an exotic world to me. I liked hearing truckers speak regional dialects, for example from the Deep South or the upper northeast. I liked imagining their gypsy-like travels that took them to far-away places. Some of them even spoke with a foreign accent. At that time, Route 15 was on one of the major truck routes from Florida to Canada. Years later, air transport would take over a share of carrying produce and other goods across the country, but in the early fifties, the trucking industry was king. Of course, there were other travelers of all kinds that stopped to get gas or eat a meal, but the truckers were our mainstay.

Daddy had me fill in wherever he needed someone. Sometimes I worked in his office, preparing the credit card slips, or writing out checks to pay the utility bills. Other times, he'd have me sweep all around the premises with a huge, brown bristled broom, or climb up on a ladder to squeegee the large picture windows in front of the business. My least favorite job was cleaning the bathrooms, but I loved the sparkling results. I had learned how to clean from my mother, who kept an immaculate house, and expected my sister and me to do our share. From the time we could hold a dishrag, we had regular chores, which increased as we got older. I felt proud of myself, at first being mommy's little helper, and later being her right-hand assistant. By then, we had a modern washing machine, but no dishwasher, garbage disposal, automatic defrosting refrigerator, or self-cleaning oven. As a result, I've never shied away from hard work.

Of all the tasks I had at the station, I liked working in the diner best. At first, I helped out in the kitchen behind the scenes, scrubbing pots in deep, stainless steel sinks, emptying trash, making sandwiches or chopping vegetables to make soup or chili, two of our regular menu items. We didn't have any automatic chopping equipment in those days, so it had to be done by hand with sharp knives. I didn't mind the carrots and celery, but the onion was a killer, making my eyes water fiercely. The large cabbage heads used for slaw were tricky to maneuver on the sharp grater. Inevitably, some of my knuckle skin wound end up in the mix.

Another job I didn't like was making up the hamburgers. First of all, I had to fetch the meat from the vault-like, walk-in cooler, which had a heavy metal door that slammed shut to keep the cold inside. Even though the door also opened from the inside, I had visions of getting stuck in there and freezing to death next to the sides of pork and beef hanging from sharp hooks. No one would have heard me yelling or pounding on the door. It was that well insulated.

Once I hauled the 20-pound package of raw ground beef up onto the counter, the process of making patties could get underway. I would use an ice cream scooper to measure the right amount of meat for one hamburger and put the ball onto a square of waxed paper on an apparatus with a flat surface and a lever to mash the meat. In principle, it looked efficient, but sometimes the paper would slip, or the meat would fall off, or the patty would be misshapen. Then I'd have to clean everything off and start over again. It was a tedious process, but I got fairly good at it with practice. There was a constant demand for hamburgers in the diner and frozen food was not considered as good as fresh.

Sometimes, as I got older, I'd help with short order cooking, mostly easy things, like pancakes, fried eggs, ham steak or pork chops. I didn't like frying T-bone steak, because I couldn't tell when it was rare, medium or well done. Of course, the deep fryer to make French fries was running at all times, day and night. I'm sure the oil was changed once in a while, but I never saw it happen. I liked the challenge of cooking, especially trying to get everything on one order to be ready at the same time so it could be served hot. Microwave ovens had not been invented yet. We had small pots on a large, gas stove to heat up side dishes, such as peas or corn, but it was usually a mad dash at the end to dish all the food up on time.

When it came time for my break, I'd wander around the kitchen to see what struck my fancy. One advantage of owning a restaurant was having so many choices and having it all free. Everything smelled so good, it was hard to decide what to eat. I'd look into the steam table and savor the aroma of the day's specials, like clam chowder or chicken and rice soup. My favorite snack was a Dagwood sandwich. I'd pile up slices of bread layered with ham, cheese, bacon, tomatoes, sliced egg, lettuce, onions, pickles and olives, then slather it with mayonnaise, mustard and ketchup. Sometimes it would be so high I could hardly get my mouth around it. My father used to quip that I ate up all his profits. Burning calories was never a problem for me, since I stayed physically active at home and at school, in addition to working at the truck stop.

One day my father asked me to fill in for one of the waitresses. It was the weekend and he didn't have enough help out front. I hesitated, thinking "What if I messed up the orders or forgot things, or tripped and spilled food on the customers?" As if reading my thoughts, my father tried to reassure me. He said he felt sure that I could do it, and said I'd be working with a nice waitress, Bonnie, who would show me what to do. I was nervous, but didn't want to let him down. I was also excited to try something new and couldn't wait to start my shift that evening.

When I arrived, Bonnie was relieved to see me, because there were several tables of people waiting to be served. She quickly told me the basics, gave me an apron and an order pad, and wished me well. Sure enough, once I got started, I forgot my nervousness and lost all track of time. The diner was an adrenaline rush when we were busy. The combination of attending to all the details like placemats, water, napkins, silverware, condiments and food, plus constantly moving back and forth to the kitchen, coffee pot, tables, dessert case, and cash register was exhausting, but we didn't notice it while it was happening. We were caught up in the frenzy of serving meals and trying to please people. When the crowd started to thin out, I was shocked to realize that it was already after midnight. I crashed into bed that night, sore, but satisfied, looking forward to doing it all again whenever Daddy needed help.

The first thing you saw when you came into the diner was a long, red, Formica counter, hugged by a row of round, padded stools that twirled with you when you sat down on them. There were square tables and chairs with curved, chrome-plated legs that could accommodate close to 50 people when full, which only happened occasionally on a Saturday night in good weather. Usually, however, we were lucky to have 20 customers at once.

Against one wall of the restaurant was a magnificent, colorful jukebox, the type that would be a collector's item today. Reds, purples, and greens swirled like dizzy rainbows around the 100-plus selection of popular hits and country-and-western music. Diners could listen to one of their favorite tunes by dropping a nickel in the slot next to the song list, or they could splurge and hear six for a quarter. After working in the diner for a while, I could sing all the songs by heart from hearing them so many times. One of my favorite singers was Slim Whitman, whose love songs, like "Indian Love Call", "Rose Marie", "The Love Song of the Waterfall" and "I Remember You" could make me swoon. An amazing vocalist and musician, his songs topped the charts for both pop and country categories for a long time.

I liked waitressing. Some of the customers could get cantankerous if you overcooked their hamburger or forgot the ketchup, but most people were pleasant and appreciative. Sometimes it was hard to tell if the truckers liked their food, because many of them were quiet souls who stared straight ahead and ate in silence. One thing they all seemed to have in common was their love of coffee. They kept us busy, keeping their cups full at all times. My father must have drunk a dozen or more cups of coffee every day as he sat with some of the regular diners to "shoot the breeze", as he called it. I loved inhaling the aroma of fresh coffee while filling the coffee pots from the large urns.

As an advertisement, my father gave out wooden nickels stamped with "Ben's", which entitled the bearer to a free cup of coffee. He was a sucker for gimmicks and silly jokes, the type to put a Whoopee cushion on your seat before you sat down. Along with their coffee, many truckers would order a slice of pie from Mrs. Smith's Bakery, which made the most delicious pies in the area. When business was slow, I ate my share, but it was hard to choose among the many kinds. In addition to the usual apple, cherry and coconut cream, there was Boston cream, lemon meringue, coconut custard, blueberry, banana cream, pumpkin, pecan and chocolate pudding pie. One flavor we didn't have back then was key lime, which didn't come along in our culinary world until many years later, probably after people started vacationing in Key West.

The most popular item on the menu by far was French fries, which would probably still be true today, if the diner still existed. I've read that the combination of salt, grease, and crunchiness is irresistible, if not downright addictive. Fries were also reasonably priced, something that kids coming in after school, or teenagers on their dates on Saturday nights could afford. Next in demand were hamburgers, followed by - strange as it seems - hot roast beef sandwiches with mashed potatoes, which have inexplicably died out over the years. At least I haven't seen the dish offered anywhere for a long time. It was an open-faced sandwich of white bread layered with slices of roast beef, accompanied by mashed potatoes and smothered with gravy, an absolutely delicious and very satisfying soul food. In those days people had no idea about saturated fat or cholesterol, and could happily enjoy such calorie-rich food. Nowadays, some customers would want gluten-free bread, free-range beef, lactose-free milk in the mashed potatoes, and gravy on the side, just not the same at all.

Tips were a rarity in the diner. Whenever I got them, I'd sink them into the jukebox, and sing along, especially during down times. I used to perform solo parts in school and church plays, and fancied myself a singer in my teenage years. For a time, I even entertained the notion of becoming a professional singer one day. I had a good voice, but my parents didn't have the money to pay for singing lessons. In college I stopped singing after my freshman year, for no particular reason, except that chorus rehearsals were long and tedious. I just got busy with other activities, thinking I could always get back to singing whenever I wanted, then was later shocked to find out that wasn't the case. When I tried singing again after a considerable hiatus, my voice sounded raspy and weak, no longer able to hit the high notes. I didn't know that singing has to be practiced regularly to maintain the voice's singing capacity. I had thought it was like swimming or riding a bike, which you could pick back up where you left off at any time. I still miss that melodious voice and have considered taking voice lessons now to try to recoup some of that ability. Maybe it's not too late.

Some of the local residents would frequent the diner for meals or to socialize over coffee. One man seemed particularly friendly to me. He would always sit at my station at the counter and say hello. He must have been in his forties, like my father. I think they once had some kind of business dealings together. One day, the man came to our house in Blue Ridge and asked to speak to my father, who wasn't at home. My mother was upstairs sleeping and didn't hear the man come in. It was daytime, but she was worn out from having worked late at the diner the night before. The man sat down in our living room and motioned for me to come over and give him a hug. Without thinking twice about it, I went over to him. He was an acquaintance of my father's, after all.

Suddenly, he pulled me onto his lap and started to compliment me on my looks. I felt awkward, but didn't want to offend him, and embarrassed, as if I was doing something wrong. I tried to move away slowly, somehow trying to salvage the situation, but his arms were snug around me. I must have been around fourteen at the time, and had never been in such a situation before. When he took my hand and tried to make me rub his leg, I realized what was going on. By then, I could feel him moving beneath my skirt. My heart started racing as I jerked my hand away from him and jumped up. I felt confused and didn't know what to do. I was shaking, but attempting to act normal, as if nothing had happened, trying to maintain some semblance of control, perhaps in the hopes that he would calm down and leave me alone. I didn't want him to get angry. I remember trying to get him out of the house, while still remaining polite, since I had always been taught to mind my manners around my elders. Mercifully, he finally left and as soon as he did, I ran sobbing upstairs to wake my mother.

Mother consoled me and said I had done the right thing, but she wished I had awakened her. She immediately called Daddy and told him about the incident. I couldn't hear what she said and Daddy never talked to me about it. The next time I was supposed to work at the diner, I hesitated to go, fearing that the man might be there. My father told me not to worry about him anymore, because he would never set foot in, or near, the truck stop again and would never bother me again. Sure enough, I never saw the man after that. I also never learned what happened to him. Even my mother would only say that "Daddy took care of it." I imagine that he did the equivalent of running the man out of town on a rail, after severely threatening his life and limbs. This was one of a number of occasions when my father would stand up for me without question.

During certain lag times at the diner, Bonnie and I would draw grids on paper and play a game of submarines with each other to pass the time, or we'd eat a snack, or gossip about boyfriends. I was particularly fond of her and always hoped she'd be working on Saturdays when I did. She was blond, a few years older than me, probably around eighteen, and had a crush on Joe, the cook. Joe was one of the more reliable cooks we had had at the diner. I didn't think he was all that cute, but he was conscientious and seemed to really like cooking. When he asked her out, she was elated. Soon they were dating regularly, and she would animatedly relate where they went and what they did on their dates. She thought she was falling in love. Every time I worked with her, I couldn't wait to hear the next installment.

I didn't have a real boyfriend yet myself, and enjoyed the vicarious thrill.

One day at work, Bonnie looked unusually serious and asked me to sit with her outside during our break. She had something to tell me. I listened wide-eyed as she told me that on their last date, she and Joe had gone "all the way." I gasped excitedly and leaned towards her, waiting for more detail. She said that it had felt strange at first, even hurt a little, but that she liked it. She said they didn't use any protection and she was worried that she might be pregnant. She also felt guilty because, as a Catholic, she was taught that sleeping with a man before marriage was a sin. I felt sorry that she was upset, but flattered that she had confided in me. I told her I would keep my fingers crossed for her.

The problem was, they kept having unprotected sex – the birth control pill had not been invented yet – and before long, Bonnie did get pregnant. As was typical back then when a little one was on the way, they got married sooner than they might have. Fortunately in their case, they seemed to really love each other. In fact, they ended up having four kids and staying together for very many years. And, using the experience they had gained at the diner, they eventually opened their own restaurant in Taneytown, Maryland.

Unfortunately, around the middle of my eighth grade, the peaceful time at Blue Ridge came to an end. The truck stop, although running fairly successfully, had become all-consuming and my father's health had declined again, leaving him exhausted and irritable most of the time. He continued to have trouble finding reliable help for the three shifts in the diner and garage, causing him to work double and triple shifts at times. Sadly, my parents started arguing more frequently again.

During one angry scene, my father inadvertently slammed the door on my mother's two little fingers, leaving them bent at the outer joint. She screamed in pain, but didn't seek medical attention, not realizing that her little fingers would never straighten out again. In subsequent arguments with my father, she would raise her hands up to show the damaged fingers, as if indicting him for his cruelty over and over again.

There seemed to be no specific reason for their fights. A careless word could set either one of them off with contempt in their voices. I felt nervous around them, never knowing what to expect, and helpless, wishing I could do something to stop the avalanche. But, deep down, I knew there was nothing I could do. They seemed to have lost every trace of affection and tenderness towards each other. Scared and sad, I watched as they headed for another break-up.

Benjamin Edward Overstreet
12-03-1911 to 4-12-1980

Daddy Says Good-bye

* * *

MY PARENTS FOUGHT SO MANY times during my childhood, that I recognized a pattern in the escalation of their arguments. First, one of them offended the other with a critical or insulting comment. Next, a stony, but usually temporary, silence engulfed the atmosphere. Then, an ever-louder build-up of hurtful remarks ricocheted between them, sending my mother to her room in tears and leaving my father shaking in rage. Sometimes, after a particularly bad argument, one of them left the house for a few hours, or even days to calm down. Several times, my mother left town for her mother's house for a number of weeks, sometimes taking my sister and me with her. The times she went alone, I missed her terribly, and worried about whether she would come back.

Evening meals could be nerve-wracking. My parents often started picking at each other over dinner, where they were in close quarters with my sister Terry and me at the table in the so-called breakfast nook, which was enclosed by walls, just off the kitchen. Terry and I could tell by their angry expressions when it wasn't safe to talk. At those times, we sat quietly on the edge of our seats, eyes downcast. I would methodically chew my food, trying to swallow over the big lump in my throat. Even when my parents both seemed relaxed, any little trigger could set them off, causing my already scant appetite to disappear. I was a skinny, sickly child, prone to frequent throat and chest infections.

Oftentimes, it was a relief when the meal was over, and Terry and I could escape to our rooms for the night, but sometimes we'd be awakened in the wee hours by our parents' yelling. Once they had gotten out their grievances towards each other, the house usually calmed down, but I would lie awake for quite some time.

I had frequent nightmares in which I was trying to run uphill to get away from a thin, green man who was chasing me, but my feet would not run. I would grasp feverishly at clumps of grass to hoist myself uphill, but I couldn't move forward. He kept gaining on me until I woke up screaming, my heart pounding. My parents would rush to my side and try to soothe me. I don't think they ever realized what was really causing those terrible dreams.

The next day would usually find my parents slowly approaching each other again, with a word about the weather or the current news, as if nothing had happened the night before. A tentative peace would have restored itself, but it couldn't be trusted. I walked on eggshells, especially around my father, because of his volatile temper.

One night, however, my parents must have reached the realization that their differences were insurmountable. I don't remember hearing them argue before I went to bed. I have no idea what happened, why after all the years together, they decided it was time to give up. Although they had separated for varying lengths of time before, they had always found a way to come back together and try again.

I was half asleep when my father came into my room and sat on the edge of my bed. "Patsy, are you awake?" He sounded sad and said he had come to say good-bye. "Your mother and I just can't seem to get along. I've tried so hard to make things right, but nothing seems to work. I just can't make her happy." He started to choke up. As much as he hated to do it, he said, he was going to leave, this time for good, and he wanted me to know he would miss me.

This startling news made my stomach churn. I felt awkward and didn't know what to say. My father had never talked to me like this before. Here he was, confiding in me about his marriage problems. I don't remember exactly what I said, probably that I was sorry he was sad, and that I would miss him, too. When I asked him where he would go, he said he didn't know yet, but he'd keep in touch. His voice was cracking now, and his tears began to fall on my pajamas. Then he hugged me and quietly sobbed on my shoulder for a few moments.

I was stunned and confused. I had never seen him so helpless before. Here was my strong, sometimes overbearing father, whose angry outbursts I feared, clearly in pain, apparently seeking comfort from me, his 14-year-old daughter. I wasn't sure what to do, but wanted to do something to make him feel better. My hands found their way around his neck, where they began patting him gently, as I heard myself saying, "That's all right, Daddy. I understand. It'll be okay."

It felt strange, this reversal of roles, with me taking care of him, as a parent would a child, but it also felt powerful. I felt proud and flattered that my father would reveal his innermost feelings to me. At the same time, I was afraid of saying or doing the wrong thing. As we hugged each other, he told me he loved me and stroked my hair one last time. I lay awake after he closed my door, and when I finally heard the gravel under his tires, I cried into my pillow for a long time.

I'm sure my father had no idea how that encounter would affect me, but he gave me an important gift that night. By showing me that he could be vulnerable, and need someone else's support, I saw a more human side to him underneath his blustery exterior, a side that showed he could be disappointed and hurt like everyone else. I gained a greater understanding of him. And for me it was a turning point to realize that by listening and caring, I could help someone else feel better.

Before that night, my father frequently intimidated me. When he was angry, his mood could be unpredictable, ranging from friendly to irritable. His harsh voice and cold, dark eyes made me feel small and helpless. But after he came to me and let his guard down, I realized there was much more to him than his angry moods. He could be sensitive, too. He still had a short fuse at times, but having seen this soft side of him, I could be more accepting of him, and less afraid.

I think the experience helped me, a budding young person who later became a therapist, to discover a calling for myself. Perhaps the most important lesson I learned was that things are not always what they seem, and that people may have another side to them, which doesn't easily show.

Cheerleader
North Hagerstown High School, 1957

High School

AFTER GRADUATING FROM ST. ANDREW'S, I attended ninth grade at South Potomac Junior High in Hagerstown, Maryland, where my mother had rented a modest apartment for herself, my sister and me. Among tears and promises to visit, I said good-bye to Sophie and Bill, who had so kindly taken me into their home to finish the eighth grade with my class. After separating from Daddy in Blue Ridge Summit, Mom had landed a job as a secretary and was now paying the bills on her own, although with difficulty. As soon as Terry finished high school, she got a job as a receptionist and was able to contribute to our living expenses.

One day, Mom was called into the guidance counselor's office with me for a meeting, which would decide my educational future, although neither of us realized it at the time. It was shortly after the beginning of the school year when an appropriate learning track for each student had to be determined and would carry over through high school. The records from St. Andrew's had not yet arrived at my new school.

Mom always dressed nicely when she went out of the house, usually in a cotton print dress with matching cardigan sweater, preferably baby blue to highlight her pale blue eyes. She could equally well have chosen light green or grey - her eyes would adapt like a chameleon to whatever shade she wore. Her lipstick and nail polish would be the same hue as one of the colors in her clothes and her medium-length auburn hair would be freshly brushed. She never forgot to powder her nose from a round compact she carried in her purse. I always felt proud of how pretty she was, as if it were a reflection on me, and this day was no exception.

Looking somewhat nervous, perhaps unsure of what was expected of her, Mom greeted the counselor and entered the office where I was already waiting on the edge of my seat. With no idea what the meeting was about, I held my breath and waited for the counselor to begin. Was there some kind of problem?

Mom and I listened intently as the counselor explained that it was time to choose which area of study I should pursue when I started high school the following year: academic, commercial, or vocational. As neither of us understood the real differences, she went on to explain each one. I could identify with vocational because it sounded active and hands-on, although carpentry and machine shop sounded like boys' subjects. Mom could identify with commercial, since that was her area of skill. She was a whiz at typing and shorthand. Mom commented on the practicality of having these concrete skills to offer when looking for a job. The counselor agreed with her, but asked more about my school background, since we had just recently moved to Hagerstown.

As soon as Mom explained that I had gone to Catholic school for four years and had always gotten good grades, the counselor's eyes lit up and she nodded her head and grinned, as if the die was now cast. When she asked whether anyone in the family had gone to college, Mom didn't seem embarrassed to say no, except for one brother-in-law. In those days, it wasn't so common for people, especially working class, to go to college. My Uncle Bob had been ahead of his time when he graduated from college as the son of a railroad man. Could the daughter of a truck stop manager also go to college one day?

What the counselor said next most likely sealed my fate for life. She said that I probably had an excellent learning base from the nuns, that more and more people were going to college nowadays, and that by putting me into the academic track, I would at least have the proper preparation, should I decide to apply to college in the future. I, for my part, didn't feel strongly either way and trusted the adults to know best. Mom hesitated a moment, then said she guessed it wouldn't hurt, and I was off in the direction of higher education, almost by accident.

Strange, how a ten-minute conversation can determine a person's future. If the counselor hadn't been as savvy as she was, I might have ended up building beautiful furniture, or heading a secretarial pool. Not that those paths would have been undesirable; on the contrary, I might have felt secure in the definite framework they provided. As it turned out, in spite of my college education, I would grapple with the question of my career for years, trying out many hats to see if one fit, always wondering if I had chosen the right one.

My initial fear of adjusting at South Potomac after the intimate class setting at St. Andrews was unfounded. I liked changing teachers and rooms after each subject and had no trouble keeping up work-wise. I did my homework without help, which was expected in those days. If I was confused about an assignment or couldn't figure it out on my own, my parents would tell me to ask the teacher. Parents did not believe in doing their child's homework with or for them. For the most part, the kids were welcoming and I made new friends with my teammates on the volleyball team. Especially Nelda and Mary Lou, who lived near me, made me feel at home. After all these years, we still see each other at reunions.

I loved gym class, where we not only learned how to run and jump and pitch and catch balls competently, but also how to dance the two-step, the jitterbug and the waltz. The teacher believed that dance was not only a social requirement, but good exercise as well. She made it easy by breaking the steps down into chalked patterns on the floor. What a surprise to find out that the waltz was simply a rhythmical square, made by facing one wall after another, counter-clockwise. I later ended up teaching dance in our basement at home to some of the guys in my class who wanted to dance at the sock hops and the prom.

My favorite athletic feat in gym class was shimmying up a thick rope to the top of the tall ceiling of the gym. It had looked impossible at first, but when one of the other girls made it to the top, I was determined to do it, too. Although I had never tried track, I surprised myself by winning a blue ribbon in the 100-yard dash at the school's track meet. But those accomplishments were outshone by one fervent coup - making the cheerleader squad.

Tryouts for cheerleader were held towards the end of the school year in our gym, a place where I felt confident. But my heart raced when I saw how many girls showed up. We were given some cheers to practice, both physically and verbally, but my memory is all a blur. I'd never wanted anything so badly before, and couldn't think straight. During each round of eliminations, I held my breath, hoping my name would not be called. As the group dwindled around me, my heart pounded in my chest. Scared as I was, I must have done well, because the next thing that registered was my name being called over the megaphone as one of the five finalists. I had made the squad! I practically floated home, then threw my books on the floor and screamed the news to my mother. "Oh, that's nice, honey," she said, having no idea that my world would have come to an end if I hadn't made it.

I'm not sure why being a cheerleader was so important to me. I must have seen them perform on television when my father watched sports. Athletic as I was, I'm sure I wanted to learn the stunts they did, but mostly I think I wanted to be in the spotlight in a cute outfit where everyone could see and admire me. My thirst for attention and popularity was all consuming. Being well liked meant I was somebody. It would be years before I tried to find out who I really was as a person, and learn to like her.

In the fall of 1955, I went into tenth grade at North Hagerstown High School, an old, three-story brick building on North Potomac Street. Since I had already made friends in ninth grade at South Potomac, I assumed I would fit right in, not realizing that those friends would soon be going to a different, newly built high school on the other end of town. Since we had moved to a house near North High right before school started, I would be staying at the old school, which meant I had to start making new friends all over again.

This school was much bigger than junior high with about 1,200 students, long corridors and confusing nooks and crannies. I felt isolated at first, but being a cheerleader gave me an automatic connection to the other cheerleaders and to our coach. Also, other students wanted to be friends with me in order to be popular by association. The problem was that I couldn't tell who liked me for myself versus my status. And, being in the public eye, I had to be nice to everyone, whether I liked them or not. Two special schoolmates, Barbara and Jane, made me feel genuinely esteemed and became life-long friends. Also, my cheerleading buddy Martha was always supportive. She was in most of my classes and taught swimming at the "Y", as I did.

Keeping up academically in high school was harder than I thought. I had to study really hard just to get B's in most subjects, and extra hard to get C's in chemistry and algebra. The days of being a top student were over. Compared to most of my classmates, many of whom came from college-educated, professional families, I didn't feel so smart anymore. They seemed to know so much, like facts about history and literature and names of famous people and places I'd never heard of. It didn't help that I spent so much time with cheerleader and basketball practice, student council and Job's Daughters. And I always tried for leadership positions in any club or activity I joined. Unlike other girls who may have been obsessed with their weight or clothes, I was obsessed with achievement. I had no awareness of this insatiable need at the time, or how it could hurt me later on. If you had asked my parents then, they would have said I was merely "well rounded."

For much of tenth and eleventh grades, my parents were separated. My mother was usually exhausted from working all day, and just wanted to relax at night during the week. Grocery shopping and laundry took up most of the weekends, but she made time to teach me how to drive. As in most things, she was a patient teacher and I learned quickly. I knew we were having a hard time making ends meet, so I got a Christmas job as a sales clerk in the ladies' clothing department of Eyerly's downtown. That assured me money to buy presents and a discount on clothes. I liked meeting all kinds of different people and helping them find outfits to suit their figures, but I soon found out that I could never work in retail. After standing on my feet for hours at a time, I was in such pain that I had to soak in the tub after work and elevate my legs. Mentally and physically, I wasn't cut out to just stand around.

Now and then, my father would pick me up for visits, which felt awkward most of the time. We seemed to be losing touch with each other, having little opportunity to play sports together like we once did. We'd go to lunch somewhere or to a park and sit on a bench to talk. Like most teenagers, I'd usually answer "fine" when he asked me how things were going, except on one particular occasion. I was worried about math class because I had lost my book and was getting behind in my assignments. The teacher had refused to give me another book, insisting that I find mine. When I told Daddy about it, he asked me for the name of the principal and the school's phone number, but he didn't tell me what he planned to do.

Sometime later, my father told me he had called the principal and, in a nutshell, told her I could not do well in school without a textbook, and it wasn't fair to deprive me of one. He said we all lose things once in a while and I shouldn't be punished for that. He never told me exactly what transpired between the principal, the teacher and him – I probably didn't really want to know the details – but it got results. The next time I had math class, the teacher handed me a new book with a list of assignments I could make up. Again, my father had stood up for me as he had often done in the past, not just in word, but also in deed. However, sometimes he would haul out the big guns when a small pistol would do, especially when he knew he was right, which embarrassed me at times, but I loved him for it.

It was in that very same math class that I had laid eyes on Chris for the first time. Tall, blond and blue-eyed, the stuff of dreams, he distracted me from the equations on the blackboard. I was smitten as never before. Whenever the teacher called on me, I stuttered, even when I thought I knew the answer. And

I was afraid to sound stupid if I got the answer wrong. When friends told me Chris liked me, too, I was overjoyed. But he was shy at first and it took him a long time to ask me out.

When the big night came, I dressed in a snug sweater that showed my modest bosom to best advantage and borrowed my sister's perfume. We went to a movie, then to a hamburger joint where everyone went after dates. I was proud to be seen with him. Home alone, I pined for him while Elvis Presley's "I Want You, I Need You, I Love You" crooned over the radio. Sometimes late at night, I'd sneak over to his house and flash the car lights in the alley by his bedroom. At sixteen, I had just passed my driver's test and drove an old, beat-up 1948 Ford that my father bought me. In the shadows away from his parents' bedroom, Chris and I would neck and pet, but not go "all the way." Nice girls didn't do that back then, and birth control had still not been invented yet.

Chris came from an upstanding, conservative Republican family, who were friendly towards me, but I wasn't sure they approved of a truck stop owner's daughter as their son's girlfriend. Truth be told, I began to get bored with him after a while. He was studious and pleasant, but the excitement had worn off. When he asked me to go steady, I turned him down so I could date other boys. He said it was all or nothing and stopped seeing me, leaving me miserable when I saw him out with someone else. I always wondered if I had made a mistake. He ended up graduating from Colgate University and becoming a successful trust officer at a bank. Years later, when we met at a class reunion, we confessed that we had never gotten over our romance, but I reminded him that we were very young back then and didn't really know each other. We hardly even knew ourselves. I said as adults we probably would not have been compatible, given the flaming Democrat that I am, and he reluctantly agreed.

When I think back among the many good high school teachers I had, one stands out, my speech teacher, Ms. Boyle. She was petite and mildly sarcastic, wore long, flowing clothes and a tight bun on the back of her head. She frequented the theaters in New York City and would tell us about the performances, some of them odd sounding, like "Waiting for Godot" or "The Postman Always Rings Twice". She liked to remind us of our uncultured ways, being as we were from the "sticks" of Maryland. But she talked down to you in that curious way that made you want to better yourself to prove her wrong.

One time shortly before Christmas, she brought in a recording of "Amahl and the Night Visitors," which she played for the entire class period. I fell in love with all of it: the story, the music, the lyrics. The passion in Amahl's young voice when he begs the three kings to let his mother go after she steals from them melted my heart and brought tears to my eyes. From then on, I listened carefully when Ms. Boyle told us about worthwhile productions. I later bought a copy of the recording of "Amahl and the Night Visitors" for myself and went to see it live on stage. I didn't know then that one day in the distant future I would take my little granddaughter Gabby to see it performed at her neighborhood theater.

Senior year was very busy for me. My parents had reunited once again, moving us into another house on North Potomac

Street right near my high school, but I didn't pay much attention to their relationship. I was caught up in my own world as captain of the cheerleaders, forward on the basketball team and queen of Job's Daughters. I wished them the best, of course, but didn't feel the same impact of the state of their marriage as I did as a child. Also, a new matter of interest was afoot among my classmates: what they were going to do after graduation. I'd hear some of them talking about colleges they had visited and where they hoped to be accepted, but my parents hadn't said anything to me about college, and they probably didn't know how to maneuver the application process. Having recently reunited once again, they were preoccupied, trying to make their marriage work.

Luckily, my friend Earl, who was a junior at the University of Maryland, encouraged me to apply for admission. He thought I had the grades to get in and brought me an application. He showed me how to get tuition assistance based on my family's income and how to get a part-time job at the front desk of the dormitory I'd live in. When my father saw that I was serious about going to college, he asked a business acquaintance, a fellow Elk and state legislator, for a partial scholarship. My parents would be able to pay for books and other incidentals. Finally, when the funding sources were all pieced together, I'd have enough to pay the fees and tuition ($15 per credit at that time!), if I got in. The day the college acceptance letter came, I could hardly contain myself. I was going to be the first one in my immediate family to go to college.

High School Graduation, 1958

Job's Daughters, Honored Queen, 1957

Job's Daughters

*   *   *

A S A YOUNG TEENAGER I was always on the lookout for a good time, usually hoping to meet cute boys, but there wasn't much going on in our small town to bring young people together. I was in 10th grade at North Hagerstown High School when I first heard of an organization called Job's Daughters, mostly from their reputation of giving fun parties, dances and hayrides. Although providing good times was certainly not the founders' main purpose for this group, the leaders seemed to know it didn't hurt to have a hook to get young girls interested. It sure worked for me, but the social aspect of my three years as a member turned out to be quite secondary to the spiritual awakening that actually took place.

Job's Daughters was the girls' branch of the Free Masons, a Christian service organization founded in the 17th century in Britain. Free Masonry then spread across the U.S., with the off-shoot for teenaged girls being established in Nebraska in 1920. The only requirement for joining was to have a relative who had belonged to the Masons. My deceased paternal grandfather,

Robert Overstreet, filled that bill for me, paving the way for my induction into Job's Daughters sometime in 1955 at the age of fifteen. After submitting an application along with letters of reference, I watched the mail hopefully until the happy day came with the good news of my acceptance.

The meetings took place in the local Masonic Lodge, a rather dreary, musty-smelling old edifice with creaky wood floors near the warehouses on the edge of town. The structure must have been important in its day, as attested by its stately, high ceilings, wide staircases and carved wood trim. Walking through the entrance made me feel like I was stepping back in history.

From the beginning, I loved the pomp and ceremony of the meetings. The members wore long, white, satiny gowns, secured around the bosom and waist with decorative cords, making them look like Greek goddesses. Some of them carried certain symbols, or sat in special chairs during the meetings, depending on their level of seniority in the group. A prescribed hierarchy dictated the order of the lineup of the girls to enter the meeting hall: first, the Honored Queen, looking majestic with the bejeweled crown on her head, followed by the other elected officials, then the newer members and, finally, the initiates. When all was ready, the chatty scurrying became a dignified quiet as the girls composed themselves. The dimmed lights and soft music bestowed a calm over the atmosphere as the large, ornate doors opened.

Dressed in my satin robe for the first time, I felt pretty and proud the day I was formally inducted. The gown swished luxuriously around my legs as I slowly marched in step to the solemn music along with the other new members into the large hall, trying to catch the eyes of my parents in the crowd of guests gathered for the ceremony. They were back together again during this time and I was happy to have them both attend one of my important functions, which had not always been the case.

The sacred objects used during the meeting, like a bell or a scepter, and the use of secret words and codes appealed to me. Even though I couldn't have explained their exact meaning in the ritual, they symbolized a mystical power that I found both intoxicating and reassuring. After the ceremony my parents received congratulations and flowers, as if I had just accomplished something important by joining this group. Over the next three years, I would discover just how meaningful my affiliation was to become.

Part of the mission of Job's Daughters was to help the less fortunate in the community. In order to strengthen our sense of compassion and generosity, we did charitable work like holiday singing at nursing homes, raising money from bake sales for children's programs, or helping with food drives, activities I had always enjoyed, harkening back to my Girl Scout days. Helping people made me feel important, and grateful for what I had.

Another part of the group's mission was to help the members develop positive character traits based on the Bible and the life of Job. According to the Biblical story, Job had been a healthy, prosperous family man with seven sons and three beautiful daughters before disasters of all kinds struck his life. One after the other, plagues and pestilence wiped out his family and business, leaving him sick, alone and destitute. In spite of his adversities, he kept his faith, accepting what he saw as the will of God. After mourning his losses, he set about working to rebuild his life. As part of our monthly meetings we read passages in the Book of Job that illustrated his acceptance, patience and hard work, all of which made sense to me; but the part that said God was testing Job's faith by subjecting him to all that pain and suffering did not make sense to me. I struggled to understand how a loving God could do this to a person, and why a benevolent God would need this kind of validation anyway.

I was pondering these heavy questions now for the second time in my young life – the first time having been at Catholic school - but found no satisfying answers. Yet, I didn't let this confusion overshadow the overall good feelings I had about participating in the group. I liked the mysteriousness of the antiquated English words of the Bible. Even when I didn't understand some of the phrases, their exotic, rhythmic sounds could put me in a tranquil, trance-like mood, reminiscent of the effect of the priest's recitations during mass at St. Andrew's, where I had sung in the choir on special occasions.

After the meetings, we usually adjourned downstairs to meet the boys from DeMolay, which was the young men's branch of the Masons. The fun and dancing certainly lived up to its reputation, as did the hayrides and cookouts, but these social events, as important as they were to me initially, took a back seat after the first year or so. A feeling of personal satisfaction began to develop gradually from doing good works and belonging to something larger than my own little world. I began to look forward to the serene state I felt during the meetings, something I rarely experienced in my busy, adolescent life and almost never at home with its frequent turmoil.

For two years, I attended the meetings faithfully, accepted different duties as they presented themselves, and filled various offices in the hierarchy, like messenger, recorder, and chaplain, on a track that would culminate in the highest, most prestigious office of Honored Queen. As Queen I would wear the lavish, purple cape and sparkling crown and would preside over meetings from the center of the elevated dais. As well as a testimony to all the dedication and effort I had put forth, this would be a dream come true. I could envision myself up there looking regal, while my parents and friends looked on.

Finally, after completing all the prerequisites, I was assigned a coach to help me prepare for my big coronation day to take place in a few months. One evening as she and I were planning the program for my ceremony, she casually asked, "By the way, Patsy, what church do you belong to?" When I answered that I didn't belong to any church, she suddenly got very quiet and stared at me. Then she said in a serious tone, "We have a problem."

She explained that eligibility to become Honored Queen required not only the completion of certain hours of service, leadership on various committees, and evidence of good character, but also membership in a Christian church. As queen, I would be expected to invite all the members of Job's Daughters to visit my church and introduce them to my pastor and congregation. I had gone to churches as part of a group under other honored queens, but didn't know that membership was an official requirement. I thought it was just a tradition. My coach sounded shocked when she said that I was the first person she had ever met at Job's Daughters who was not a member of a church.

I panicked. What should I do? I had been so excited about becoming Honored Queen, and had worked so hard for it. Now my big dream was threatened by what seemed to be an unfair technicality. To think, I could be deprived of my hard-earned position, just because I didn't belong to an organized church. What difference did it make, as long as I tried to live by decent values and be a good person? I was still myself, regardless of a church affiliation. It was frustrating, not to be accepted for my own merits.

My parents commiserated with me, but didn't know how to help. Beyond the few scattered times my mother had taken my sister and me to Sunday school, we had never been much of a church-going family and certainly weren't members anywhere. On Sundays, Daddy preferred sleeping in and reading the paper leisurely over his coffee, rather than getting dressed and going somewhere at a certain time. Having been raised Baptist, he would sometimes quote the Bible to emphasize a point in a discussion, but rarely went to church.

Part of me wanted to fight this injustice and give up the post as designated queen in protest. But that would be hurting myself. I anguished back and forth about it, but my heart, my soul and, yes, my ego connived to overpower the principle of the matter, and I began scrambling around to find a church.

I started visiting Sunday services at a few friends' churches, trying to find one where I felt reasonably comfortable. After some weeks of attending various protestant churches, including Lutheran, Methodist, and Baptist, I finally settled on one that seemed moderate in its views, and gave the name and address to my mentor. I stated simply that this was the church we would be visiting during my upcoming tenure as queen. She seemed relieved, and didn't push for further details, thank goodness, because I never officially joined that church; I only chose it for the purpose of satisfying the requirement. On one hand, I felt somewhat guilty for doing it, but on the other, I thought my actions were justified because their requirement was so unfair.

When my mentor gave me the go-ahead, I breathed a sigh of relief and dove into the preparations for my big day. Much like planning a wedding, there were invitations to print, color themes to choose, menus and table decorations to decide, gifts and corsages to purchase. I didn't mind doing most of it myself, as I wanted everything just so. My mother was to get a small spray of pink carnations to pin on her suit jacket, while my father would sport his bright boutonniere. In a way, these secular preparations were a distraction from the real mission of Job's Daughters, but for a seventeen-year-old this was a big deal and I could hardly contain myself.

After weeks of bustling around, attending to a thousand details, the night of my coronation finally arrived. Up until the music for the procession intoned, I was worried about whether I had forgotten anything, whether the ceremony would go off as planned, and whether I would forget my lines. But as soon as I heard the familiar sounds of our regular marching music, the peaceful calm I had come to expect washed over me and I was able to let go and accept whatever came.

Just as I entered the softly lit room, I saw my parents in the front row, beaming proudly at me. Surrounding them were Masonic members, their families and guests to witness the special, annual event. As custom dictated, the out-going queen placed the purple cape around my shoulders and the stately crown on my head, the tangible culmination of two years of effort and dedication. It was a delicious moment of basking in my accomplishments, even as I felt the weight of responsibility facing me for the coming year as queen.

At the end of the crowning, I was showered with warm congratulations as we made our way down to the party room. Everything went without a hitch. The food and company couldn't have been better. My parents seemed to glow as they spoke to the other guests about their daughter. I hated to see the magical evening end.

While visiting the churches before my coronation, I noticed something troubling. It seemed that each church had a different slant on religious questions, such as the meaning of God, Christ, the Holy Spirit, sin, salvation and the hereafter, yet each church seemed certain in their own interpretations, claiming to have the right answers, just like the nuns at St. Andrew's had done. I also noticed the differing, sometimes conflicting, structures of dogma, which further confused me. The ones that preached eternal damnation were particularly scary. If I had been skeptical about organized religions to begin with, this experience only strengthened my doubts about joining a church in the future. Spirituality, however, would always remain important to me. Living by decent values, caring for others, and trying to reduce the pain in the world would become my guiding principles.

My misgivings about church membership, however, didn't diminish my fondness for Job's Daughters. During my three years there, I had deepened my social consciousness and developed an appreciation for ritual and tranquility. Although I wasn't aware of it at the time, it was here that I first experienced the calming components of meditation. To this day, I love the sound of a gong drawing a hushed veil of silence over a group, or the warmth of soft lights as music begins a procession, or an inspiring invocation that soothes the soul.

The fun-loving, adventure-seeking young girl who first entered that Masonic temple looking for a good time emerged more mature and more compassionate, with a deeper understanding of values, social issues and serenity. Job's Daughters filled a need for my budding spirituality, which I hadn't even known was there.

My Parents after my Installation Ceremony as Honored Queen

Minnie Rebecca Payne (Mildred) Love
5-28-1899 to 3-20-1982

My Grandmother Mildred

* * *

As a child, I never knew much about my grandmother Mildred, except what I experienced first hand from time spent with her. As an adult, I found out that she was only fourteen years old when she gave birth to my mother in Booie, North Carolina, probably in or around 1915, a time when such a circumstance was surely a scandal, especially among country folk. The year may not be correct, as I heard this from my mother, who tended to skimp on her age by a couple of years. This, like most personal information about Mildred, was supposed to remain secret. She was always a very private person, sometimes verging on paranoid, which got worse as she aged.

It seems incredible to me now to realize that I know nothing about Mildred's parents, who would have been my great grandparents, or any other relatives she may have had, for that matter. I only know that she must have spent some of her youth in Booie, a small, rural town near the Appalachian Mountains, where my mother was born. As a teenage mother,

Mildred must have had help raising my mother and my Uncle Otis, who was born two years later, but I have no idea from whom. If there were aunts, cousins, or friends, say, Mildred must have lost contact with them, as she never talked about them.

My mother had only vague memories of her father, George Binam, who was said to have been gored to death by a bull in a field when she was very small. I'm not even sure that really happened, because as I got older, I realized that Mildred sometimes fabricated things, too. I often wondered how Mildred had met my grandfather. Did she have a crush on him, or were other forces at play? According to my baby book, where my mother filled out the family tree, he was three years older than Mildred and from the same area, Wilkes County, North Carolina. I don't remember asking my grandmother any questions about him or her family, which would have been normal for most children to do as a child. I must have sensed that personal questions were taboo. Whenever I asked my mother about her father, she repeated the bull story, but little else. Maybe she really didn't remember much about him, or she didn't want to say what she knew.

There were few photographs in Mildred's house. I remember one hanging on the wall of a man in a Navy uniform, perhaps from World War II. Maybe he didn't return from the war. Mildred never mentioned him, and I never saw any men's things around the house. I did see some items that suggested foreign places, perhaps gifts to her, like a coconut whittled into a happy face, an exotically patterned shawl with long fringes, and a hula lamp. I wonder what led to Mildred's secretiveness. Maybe people had abandoned her early in life, making her mistrustful, or maybe she was a loner by nature. I don't know if she had ever married. I feel sad to realize that I will never know the answers to these mysteries. All the people who might have known more about her have surely long since died.

Mother used to take Terry and me with her to Mildred's place when she and my father separated, which was at least every couple of years. Even though the circumstances were upsetting, I always looked forward to visiting Mildred, if only to get some respite from my parents' arguments. She would hug us when we arrived, but was otherwise not very affectionate. Much of the time she seemed preoccupied, perhaps worried about my mother. The two of them would sit at the kitchen table, chain-smoking Pall Malls and drinking coffee for hours while talking with serious demeanor. I knew Mother was trying to decide what to do each time, whether to go back to my father, or let this time be the final break. A similar scenario repeated itself in Norfolk, Virginia, and Milwaukee, Wisconsin, from the time I was around five years old throughout grade school. Each time, my mother returned to my father, usually after a few weeks when her money ran out. In those years, before she went to secretarial school, she wouldn't have been able to support herself.

Mildred had never liked my father and wanted my mother to leave him for good, but she had no income to help us either, beyond some kind of welfare available in those days, the early to late forties. I don't know why she didn't get a job, perhaps because of her multiple physical complaints, or because she didn't get along well with other people.

When we'd arrive for a visit, Mildred's refrigerator was usually almost empty. At its most meager, her cupboard housed little more than peanut butter and coffee, but in good times, there were Vanilla Wafers or Fig Newtons, my favorites. Breakfast usually consisted of cereal or sometimes eggs. Orange juice and bacon were a luxury. Lunch was usually bologna sandwiches, slathered with mayonnaise, but no lettuce or tomatoes. Dinner could be a hamburger patty, boiled potatoes and canned peas. Paltry as it was, Mildred gladly shared whatever she had. If she could spare some change, Terry and I would each have a Popsicle from the ice cream truck for dessert.

Many a time, while my mother was still with my father, I saw her secretly stick a five-dollar bill in with a letter to Mildred. She would squirrel away a little money from her grocery allowance when my father wasn't looking. My Uncle Otis apparently lived with Mildred much of the time, often out of work, or on an alcoholic binge, unable to help much financially. I heard my mother say he was a die caster by trade – I've never known exactly what that was - and could have earned well, if not for the drink.

Otis was a handsome guy who liked to laugh, and brightened the atmosphere when he was there during our visits. He was more open, but he knew Mildred didn't like the neighbors snooping, so he told me what to do if any of them started to ask me personal questions. He said I should stare at them, drop my jaw open, and say a long, drawn out, "huuuuh?" Then, walk away!

Mildred tended to speak in quick starts and hushed tones, her eyes often darting sideways. She rarely smiled. Since she was always nice to me, though, I wasn't exactly afraid of her, just a bit wary. I remember quietly testing the mood between my mother and Mildred when the two were talking. They didn't always see eye to eye, and tensions could erupt without warning, even though my mother tended to defer to her. I knew not to interrupt or make noise when their heads were huddled together.

Sometimes I felt bored at Mildred's house. I tried to busy myself reading comic books, playing jacks on the floor, or practicing crocheting or tatting, which Mildred had taught me. She was a patient teacher and would unravel good-naturedly the mistakes I'd make with my beginner's attempts. A whiz with a crochet needle, she created intricate designs for elaborate doilies, which adorned the arms and backs of her old-fashioned upholstered furniture. My favorite was a pineapple motif with scalloped edging. She seemed most relaxed when her fingers were flying. After much perseverance, I did acquire some skill, and completed small doilies for end tables or miniature snowflakes to hang on the Christmas tree, a far cry from the gorgeous, large bedspreads Mildred made.

At Mildred's house there was usually no one to play with and television would not be invented for another five years, at least not for home viewing. My sister, being four years older, was just beyond the reach of the toys and games that interested me. Plus, I was a tomboy and she loved staying inside with fashion magazines. Mildred didn't have her own yard, but I would climb the trees behind her apartment building, beg a soda from the guys who worked at the Coca Cola factory down the street, or wander off exploring the area. In summer, I went mostly barefoot, dodging the broken glass on the sidewalks of her neighborhood. If I cut myself, Mildred or Mom would automatically fetch the Mercurochrome and a Band-Aid, but not make me put my shoes on. Kids were supposed to go barefoot in summer - I just needed to be more careful. I don't remember Mildred ever fussing at me about anything. She treated me gently, perhaps recognizing my vulnerability amid my parents' difficulties, and the frequent instability they caused in my childhood.

When Mildred lived in Norfolk, her house was near a municipal art museum. I discovered it on one of my forays to escape her smoky kitchen and, at around age eight, began my love affair with fine art. I admired the beautiful paintings on the walls, the decorative vases in lighted display cabinets, the exotic African sculptures, and colorful woven textiles placed strategically under special spotlights. The deliciously air-conditioned rooms, rare in those times, enveloped me like a cool breeze. I must have stayed for a long time that first visit, lost in the mesmerizing visual buffet.

When Mildred and my mother asked me where I had been, they seemed surprised, but not worried. Each time I went back, I found something new to admire. Thinking back now, it was probably not safe for me to have been alone in that museum. There were hardly any visitors on weekdays and only a few guards. But in those days, parents were not as concerned as they are nowadays about kids walking around on their own.

According to my mother, Mildred had been a hairdresser as a younger person and had quite a store of knowledge about natural remedies for hair and skin care. She taught my mother the vinegar rinse trick to make hair shiny and more manageable. Conditioners had not been invented yet. Mildred brushed her long, auburn hair daily, at least 50 strokes, and let it hang loosely around her shoulders for every day. On special occasions, she'd twist it on top of her head over a wire mesh piece to give it more height, fastening it carefully with long hairpins. Now and then, she would use henna for highlights.

Mildred prided herself on her looks, never leaving the house without lipstick. To remove the nicotine stains, Mildred soaked her nails in a lemon solution and filed them regularly with an emory board. She was a slender, attractive woman like my mother. When people exclaimed how they looked like sisters, Mildred did not bother to correct them. They both had good figures and dressed as nicely as they could, given their limited means.

Some of my fondest memories of Mildred were the times we went to the beach. Since she couldn't afford an automobile, the four of us would pile into the rickety streetcar and head for Virginia Beach, about an hour's ride away. There was no air conditioning in public transportation back then. The narrow windows of the hot trolley couldn't make a dent in the swelter. In spite of the shorts and halter-tops my sister and I wore, the backs of our thighs still got sweaty and sometimes stuck to the wooden slats of the seats. Mother and Mildred would wipe their dripping brows, sighing in unison about the humidity. They loved the beach as much as we did and couldn't wait to catch the ocean breeze.

When I could finally see the ground getting sandier and the pine trees getting denser, I knew we'd be there soon. I could almost smell the salt sea air. The tall Ferris wheel in the distance meant that we were approaching Ocean View, the amusement park right next to the beach. Mother and Mildred took us there one evening when they were meeting two sailors in a bar on the boardwalk. They introduced Terry and me to the men, gave us some money, and told us to go on some of the rides for a while.

I don't remember what my sister did, but I ended up scaring myself by going into the haunted house alone. I must have been around seven or eight years old. There were slanted floors and wavy mirrors that made me dizzy, bloody faces and skeletons that jumped out at me, while chains rattled near my ears. The worst part was a section like a labyrinth, in which I got disoriented and began to panic. When I finally found my way out, I ran back to the bar, panting and pale.

Mother and Mildred didn't seem happy to see me back so fast, but I was afraid to go out alone again. Apparently, they had been enjoying themselves and were smiling in a flirty way at the sailors. I felt awkward sitting at the table with the adults, clearly interfering with their good time. I don't know whatever became of the sailors, because when my mother went back to my father, they were never mentioned again. Of course, I was told not to tell my father anything that went on when we stayed at Mildred's. I hated being asked to keep secrets from him. It made me feel like I had something to be ashamed of.

I loved going into the ocean with my mother, who would hold me on her hip and ride the waves. She was her happiest then, giggling and jumping up and down. For some reason, I don't remember Mildred going into the water except to wade. She probably didn't want to mess up her hair, or maybe she couldn't swim. She and Mother had contests to see who could bend over the farthest to touch their toes in the sand while keeping their legs straight. Mildred was most proud of her flexibility, and usually took the prize.

For lunch we bought the cheapest things available, usually hot dogs, and loaded them with the free onions, relish and French's mustard from the counter. If there was enough money, we'd share a coke and a bag of potato chips. I was left feeling hungry at times – swimming has always made me ravenous - but the fun of the day smothered the pangs.

I remember getting terrible sunburns at the beach, where there was no shade and we couldn't afford to rent an umbrella. Terry and I wore tee shirts to protect us, but it wasn't enough. It's a wonder we didn't get skin cancer, because we didn't use sunscreen back then. At the end of the day, we dragged back home on the trolley, lobster-red and exhausted, but content. At bedtime, I used Mildred's remedy of full strength vinegar on the painful places, followed by gobs of Noxzema to cool the burning.

Mildred used to let me play with her jewelry. She kept it in a large jewelry box lined with red felt. There were bright beads, shiny chains and strings of pearls, all costume jewelry, of course, but rich-looking to me. She had sparkling rings and silver bracelets, earrings of all shapes and sizes, even decorative hatpins. She had large brooches, some in animal or flower designs made with bright, colored stones. I would take the pieces gently from the box, lay them on her bed and try them on, one by one. Mildred also let me dress up in some of her old clothes. I particularly liked the ones from the flapper age and would pick out the longest beads to wear with them. She and Mother would smile at my get-ups. Mildred trusted me to put everything back carefully and never checked up on me.

As I got older and we moved several times, I lost touch with Mildred. I knew from my mother how she was doing, but I seldom wrote to her myself, except maybe a card at Christmas. We didn't call long distance, because it was very expensive and Mildred usually had no phone, anyway. When my mother hadn't heard from her in a long time, she would try to reach a neighbor and have Mildred called to the phone.

Mildred came to visit us once in Blue Ridge Summit when I was around thirteen, but that ended badly when Daddy blew up at one of her sarcastic remarks and asked her to leave. I remember thinking she was acting somewhat odd, like mumbling under her breath and frequently rummaging through her purse, which made me feel uncomfortable around her. Since we hadn't seen each other for a long time, she was almost like a stranger to me. Still, she was my grandmother and I thought I should feel closer to her than I did. But in spite of feeling guilty, I ended up staying outside as much as possible to avoid the tension in the house until she left.

Years later, when I was in college, Mother lost track of Mildred for a while and was worried. Finally, she learned that Mildred was hospitalized on the psychiatric unit of a nursing home in Williamsburg, Virginia. We didn't know how she had come to be admitted, or how long she had been there. The nurse only knew that she acted paranoid and needed supervision. I drove Mother there, fearful of what we might find.

When we first spotted Mildred, I gasped and my mother covered her mouth with her hand, momentarily speechless. She had lost so much weight, we hardly recognized her. She was disheveled, but clean, and wore a drab housedress. Her hair had turned grey and her eyes looked vacant. She was sitting on the edge of her cot in a large ward with only a low wall to divide her small space from the many others.

This was my first encounter with a mental ward and I felt afraid. Some of the patients looked menacing; others came up too close and stared; some had bizarre body movements. Low moans could be heard rising up from some of the beds. The dull, green paint of the cinder block walls mingled with urine odor to turn my stomach. Mildred clutched a plastic bag with her belongings tightly on her lap. I wanted to get out of there as soon as possible and suggested we go out somewhere for a bite to eat.

The three of us went to a nearby diner, but no one had much appetite. Mildred was agitated and confused. When it came time to go back to the hospital, she got upset, because she had thought we were taking her home with us. With heavy hearts and many assurances that we would be back soon, Mother and I left her there, looking dejected. Mother felt so guilty that she arranged to move Mildred in with her shortly thereafter without telling my sister or me, but was not able to take care of her. Mildred ended up going back to another nursing home, this one farther away, in the southern part of West Virginia, where we never saw her again. I assume she was on Medicaid at the time and was sent to the nearest facility with a Medicaid bed available. She may not have been cognizant enough to give the staff all her family's contact information, or she may have lost it. Otherwise, the staff would have informed my sister and me that she was there.

The following year, while helping my mother move into an assisted living facility in Charles Town, West Virginia, I came across a letter advising her of Mildred's death. It was postmarked a few months earlier, but Mother hadn't told me about it. Mother's health had been failing, both physically and mentally, and she was often confused and forgetful. In fact, I now believe that she had early onset of Alzheimer's disease. Also, she may have been in shock when she got the news of Mildred's death, and possibly overcome by remorse that she had not been able to provide her a home.

I felt sad for Mildred, dying so far away from family, and hoped she hadn't suffered. The letter stated that she had died of "natural causes," a catchall term used back then when doctors weren't sure of the diagnosis. She had had a hard life, living in poverty, and raising two kids with little support and few opportunities. She was often isolated and probably lonely, but there is one thing that I know she did very well: she was a nice grandmother to me as a young girl. She made me feel loved and accepted. She showed me attention and caring, as far as she was able, and taught me a lot about needlework. To this day, every time I crochet something, I think of her. I hope in some small way that I gave her joy during our visits, and made her feel important, too.

Part Two
On My Own

* * *

Part Two
On My Own

First Year at the University of Maryland

* * *

EXCITEMENT FILLED THE AIR, AS car after car discharged freshmen in front of their assigned dormitories on move-in day. Mine was St. Mary's hall, the oldest, quaintest one on campus. Ivy-covered and red-bricked, it had imposing Greek columns in the front like all the other buildings, sophisticated and proper-looking. The inside also had its standards of propriety with tastefully upholstered Queen Anne chairs for visitors, who were only allowed on the ground floor. They had to sign in at the front desk and have the resident's room number buzzed on the intercom to announce them.

My parents helped me carry my things inside while I expectantly clutched the name of my future roommate, Ginny, who had been given to me by lottery. We ascended the stairs to my room on the second floor, where Ginny had already been unpacking. Her warm smile welcomed me to the 10' X 18' space we would share for the coming year. After our belongings were stowed in the scant cupboards, it was time for all the parents to leave. I didn't mind saying good-bye, as I was already beginning to feel at home. While dating Earl during my senior year in high school, I had spent some weekends on campus, and had gotten used to the huge expanse of rolling lawns and courtyards around the many buildings of the university.

From the start, Ginny and I meshed in many ways, with similar routines and study habits. Luckily, she was happy on the top bunk, while I preferred being closer to the ground. We often ate together in the dining hall and studied quietly in our room. Working creatively with red ribbon and tin foil, we won first prize for the most beautifully decorated holiday door in the dorm that December. We confided in each other about our worries and fears, and, before long, became fast friends, sometimes visiting each other's families on weekends. It was through visiting her at her home in Annapolis that I came face-to-face with alcoholism, her mother's alcoholism. I had seen my mother abuse alcohol for periods of time, but had never met a full-blown, chronic alcoholic, which was very different and very sad.

First of all, there was never any food in the refrigerator, which meant Ginny and I had to buy groceries right after we arrived. Secondly, her mother spent most of the time in her bedroom, claiming to be ill with a headache, stomachache or other ailment. There were unpleasant odors coming down the hallway and stains trailing on the rug. Dust balls and cobwebs collected in the living room. When she did emerge, she stumbled around and slurred her speech. Sometimes she would call out angrily, ranting at Ginny about some nonsensical grievance, and Ginny would try to appease her, still trying to win her mother's approval. Ginny's father had left when she was young, probably because of her mother's drinking, and she suffered from low self-esteem. I missed Ginny when she didn't come back the following year and we slowly lost touch. Years later, I found her again and visited her, now married and a new mother. She seemed quite happy, and we vowed not to lose contact this time. But, as often happens, especially when our friends live far away, time has a way of severing ties.

My father's words had stuck with me when he asked why I would go to college if I didn't know what I wanted to study. Without meaning to, I'm sure, he sounded somewhat reproachful, which made me scramble to find a major right away. At the time, I didn't know that many freshmen like me had no idea what course of study they wanted to take, at least not at first, and took a variety of classes to find out where their interests lay.

With very little knowledge about what career might suit me, both intelligence-wise and personality-wise, I latched onto physical therapy, which seemed to fit both my desire to help people and to be physically active. I'm not sure how the idea came up. No one had suggested it and I didn't know much about it, except that I knew my high school friend, Jane, had received physical therapy after a swimming accident, which left her partially paralyzed. After many treatments I saw her graduate from a wheelchair to crutches. On the face of it, physical therapy seemed like an excellent choice for me, until I learned more about it.

To begin with, the curriculum consisted of mostly science classes. Except for a few prerequisites like English and health, the line-up was intimidating: algebra, chemistry, zoology and, what would become the bane of my studies, physics. Although I had liked my high school science classes, I had done better in the humanities, and I had never had physics before. At that time, physical therapy majors had to take a year of regular, college physics, not adapted physics, which I understand is now the case.

The first physics class is still a blur to me. I arrived on time and sat expectantly with my sharpened pencil poised. As was my custom, I thought if other people could learn a subject, so could I. After all, my father had always told me I could do whatever I put my mind to, but he had never taken college courses. Almost immediately, I felt swamped. The professor moved quickly through the material, perhaps assuming that most of the students had had high school physics, leaving little time or opportunity for questions. I probably wouldn't have dared to ask anything anyway, certainly afraid of sounding stupid, but mainly because I didn't understand enough to even formulate a question. That day, and many days thereafter, I left the class practically in tears, even after my friend Earl started to tutor me.

Earl was majoring in physics and tried his best to help me with my homework. But each of our sessions ended in utter frustration for him and me. Thinking he wasn't explaining things in a way that I could understand, I got angry with him, prompting him to get mad at me. After a few months of this debacle, we called the tutoring off, since it wasn't helping. I continued to read the textbook and attend classes, but barely passed the exams. This did not bode well for my major.

In the meantime, we P.T. majors met once a week to go on field trips to visit P.T. departments in area hospitals and clinics, as a way to introduce us to our future work. Our first outing was to an old hospital, which had its P.T. department way off in a corner of a dingy basement. Rusty pipes skirted the low ceilings, while flaking radiators clanked and hissed out too much heat. In a large, windowless room patients with sullen faces, many of them stroke victims, half-heartedly pushed or pulled levers as directed, while staff encouraged them to keep trying. Other patients, some of whom had broken their hips, were practicing ambulation with walkers, while staff held their waistbands from behind. Amputees were being fitted for prostheses. I felt claustrophobic and depressed. I don't know what I was expecting exactly, maybe a more cheerful surrounding and less incapacitated people, but I began to question whether I was cut out for this work.

Our mentor assured me that, over time, I would get used to the atmosphere and gain satisfaction from focusing on each patient. But subsequent visits to other P.T. departments weren't any better. At the end of each one, I couldn't wait to get out into the fresh air. I felt compassion for the patients, many of whom made progress in painstakingly slow increments, but gradually realized that I didn't have the fortitude or endurance required for the profession. Ultimately that recognition, in addition to my difficulties learning physics, led me to change majors.

In a way, I felt like I was giving up on something, which was unlike me, but I also felt tremendous relief. I wouldn't have to make those awful field trips anymore, nor would I have to register for physics again. However, now I had to figure out what else I wanted to study. I knew I wasn't drawn to teaching or home economics, two of the most common majors for females in those days. But since I had no idea what to do, I signed up for liberal arts to give myself more time to decide, taking mostly English literature and comparative literature classes, and hoping that something fitting would eventually come along for me.

No Books

*   *   *

I GREW UP IN A HOUSE with virtually no books, aside from a small, outdated dictionary and a Bible, but no reference books and no newspapers delivered to our house. Daddy read Dell murder mysteries in paperback that cost 25 cents each at the local drug store. He would sometimes give me a dollar and ask me to buy him a few of them. When I'd say I was afraid I might buy him ones he had already read, he'd say it didn't matter because they were all alike anyway! I think he used them as an escape from work, where he sometimes had to pump gas, change oil, and fix tires himself when some of his employees didn't show up for work. Reading seemed to relax him, regardless of the subject matter. At times he would nod off in his chair, his hands lax next to the book in his lap, snoring loudly.

Mom subscribed to "Reader's Digest", which she read cover to cover every month. Not much for reading novels, she enjoyed the condensed human-interest stories, the vocabulary test and the jokes. She also received "Horoscope" and read the daily predictions for her astrological sign, Virgo, usually in her bedroom with the door closed. She looked sheepish if anyone walked in on her reading her horoscope, as if she were doing something sneaky. When asked, she'd say she didn't really believe in astrology, but she thought it couldn't hurt to be fore-warned, just in case.

As a child, my reading material at home was paltry: a few Golden books and later some comic books. One of my favor-ites was "The Little Engine That Could". I rooted for the toy train to beat the odds and was overjoyed when his faith and hard work paid off. He became a role model for me. I'm sure my father meant well when he told me I could do anything I chose in life, but, like most kids, I needed help in figuring out what career path suited my intelligence, aptitude and personal-ity. I wish my parents had given me more direction, but I don't believe they knew how.

In high school my ignorance of books didn't seem to mat-ter initially. It wasn't cool for girls to show book smarts anyway. I just wanted to fit in and make friends. In tenth grade I wor-ried mainly about how to be popular and how to get invited to the prom. By junior year, however, I noticed that many of my classmates, boys and girls, talked about books I'd never heard of, especially during English class, and reaped positive atten-tion from teachers. I felt left out and started to read more, but it wasn't until college that I realized how deficient I was.

Soulmate Judy, 1960

Soulmate Judy

WHEN WE FIRST MET, JUDY seemed rather quiet and introverted, much different from me, so I thought. Our freshman year, she had roomed with another student, who, like my roommate Ginny, didn't return for sophomore year, so we decided to room together. As we got to know each other better, we discovered how compatible we actually were. We were both easy-going and liberal, but could be outspoken in our views, especially when it came to women's issues, civil rights and social justice. We confided in each other about boys, our parents, and secret longings. We drank Constant Comment tea and, during exam time, ordered pizza to our room late at night.

Judy and I both worked part-time at McKeldin Library on campus, shelving books and checking them out for patrons. I loved the quiet of the stacks where we put the books back in alphabetical order. Judy had a way of holding a book tenderly in her hands, as if it were a fragile object worthy of her respect. She was an English major from the start, whereas I, not knowing what else to do, had just changed my major to English. She especially loved the poets Shelley and Keats, but her real passion was art, which was her minor. I can still see her on the floor of our dorm room, hunched over a watercolor painting, not minding the inevitable drips on her clothes, and she was forever trying to clean paint from under her fingernails.

Judy didn't wear make-up and didn't need it. Her creamy clear skin and long, dark eyelashes came naturally. She didn't date much, until she met Tim, a fellow lit major, who impressed her with his poetic soul. She tells me that he still writes sonnets to this day. Back then, I thought he was kooky and immature, although not bad looking. However, he was very helpful to me once. At my request, he suggested a reading list of books for me that he considered must-reads, like *You Can't Go Home Again*, *Madame Bovary* and *Anna Karenina*. I had felt woefully behind in my knowledge of literature, and chipping away at that list got me somewhat caught up on reading. All I had needed was a place to start. Now I can hardly go to sleep at night without first reading a book for a while. Oftentimes, in fact, I'll be reading several books at a time, left in various parts of the house.

After Judy and I graduated college and moved away from each other, she met and married an Englishman and moved to England to live permanently. I visited them once and was happy to see that Judy was still doing her art. She had become surprisingly original, albeit brash, in some of her paintings, for example drawing upright penises for gateposts of a garden. She was also most fanciful with some pictures. My favorite was a jungle scene that looked like a tangle of trees and vines at first glance, but a closer look revealed many delightful, gnome-like creatures peeking from behind the plants.

During my visit, I slept under some creative quilts Judy had pieced together from scraps of soft velvet, shiny silk and fuzzy cotton, and was reminded of the time in college when she whipped up a dress for me over a weekend at her parents' house and surprised me with it. Flowing and comfortable, it was a simple moo-moo, which was all the rage at the time. No matter that the seams weren't straight, I cherished her labor of love.

Once, when Judy was facing surgery, I jokingly agreed to come to London to help her if she would teach me to water-color in return. I had just started taking art classes and needed some pointers. Judy took me up on my offer and said she'd teach me to paint ducks, her favorite subject. In just a week, she taught me to paint three distinctively different kinds of ducks, progressive in difficulty. The first was a plain, white and rust colored one; the second, a fat, red polka-dotted one with more character; and the third, a blaze of riotous feathers from head to toe. Unlike me, Judy knew the elaborate names of all of them, both in English and Latin.

An excellent and patient teacher, Judy told me to look care-fully at the photographs of the ducks, using a magnifying glass if necessary, to really see the details before painting. At the same time, she allowed me just enough room for experimenta-tion that I felt my renditions were original. In the end, I was amazed at my three creations and framed them when I got home. I've been doing watercolor paintings ever since.

To protect her clothes during our painting sessions, Judy wore a pretty, cotton smock, which she had sewed herself. I joked how the smock made her look like a real Bohemian artist, like something out of "La Boehme." When I hinted that I'd like to have one, too, she offered to sew me one similar to hers, and, about two weeks later, a small package arrived with the most wonderful, artsy-looking smock in brightly colored stripes, with a gathered bodice and wide sleeves, just perfect for painting. I love wearing that smock for inspiration when I paint and as a heart-warming reminder of our life-long friendship.

Mt. Snow

* * *

SHIRLEY, ONE OF MY DORM mates at St Mary's Hall, and I had become ski bums of sorts, as much as anyone could while living in the mid-Atlantic state of Maryland, where we didn't have consistent snowfalls each winter to support the sport. Having taken several local trips to White Tail and Round Knob together to "do" the slopes, the white bunny had bitten us, but the trails of Maryland resorts frequently consisted of man-made snow, which was grainy or icy. We longed for a decent mountain with higher chair lifts and long runs to make all the rented paraphernalia and lift tickets worthwhile. Since she didn't have a car, I did all the driving in the Ford Fairlane my father had bought me.

Shirley and I were around 20 years old, juniors living down the hall from each other in St. Mary's Hall. We had a very strict "house mother" with an eagle eye, that saw and punished every minute we came in after curfew. Before leaving the dorm to go out, we had to write down the exact time of departure, the name of our date, if we had one, and the destination with the contact name and phone number of the person we were visiting. Upon our return, we had to sign back in, noting the time. Each day of the week had its own curfew, with Friday and Saturday at 12:30 a.m. Purportedly, these measures were the school's attempt to protect its young women, but if we had wanted to get into any mischief, we could certainly have done it before curfew as well as after. The men's dorms had no curfew. They were free to get into as much mischief as they liked.

The only way men could gain access to the upper floors of the women's dorms was during a so-called "panty raid", when a hoard of them would gather near the men's dorms and race toward a selected women's dormitory, hoping to catch the women unawares - that is, with the doors unlocked – and run upstairs to steal a clutch of panties from their rooms. If successful, they'd flaunt their booty by waving it high above their heads like flags of conquest as they retreated to their quarters. If we got word that a raid was coming, we'd lock the doors to thwart their efforts. Once, I got my picture on the front page of "The Diamondback," the campus newspaper, showing me pulling the heavy front door shut just seconds before the raiders arrived. I was actually scared and my adrenaline was pumping, as if I were saving our dorm from certain disaster, but it was all in good fun. Strangely, it never occurred to us to raid the men's dorms for their underwear. Maybe we had better things to do.

As hall mates, Shirley and I hung out in a group with our respective roommates, neither of whom liked sports. So the two of us would take off on a Saturday morning and try to hit the slopes by early afternoon, ski our hearts out for a few hours, and then drive back in the evening. Once we tried night skiing under floodlights, but the black sky chilled the air, and we missed the views. Besides, it didn't feel right, like we were forcing something against nature. What crazy person would ski in the dark anyway?

Before long, we were itching to conquer new territories when one of us heard about Mt. Snow, a popular ski resort in Vermont that had months of consistently good, skiable snow. We were dying to go there but it was so far and hotels were expensive. Then a friend told us that some hotels traded waitressing help for free meals and cots to sleep on. Since Shirley and I both had been waitresses, we thought we'd give it a try. On a whim, we took off one Thursday and headed north, planning to sort things out when we arrived.

We must have driven about 18 hours in two days, stopping at a cheap bed and breakfast for the night. It seemed to take forever, but seeing the snow get deeper and deeper on the side of the road gave us joyful anticipation of perfect skiing. Early on Friday afternoon, we cheered when we finally saw the first sign for Mt. Snow.

Having never been to a real winter resort before, I was delighted to see the charming A-frame lodges with massive, stone fireplaces and large, après-ski lounges that looked onto the ski slopes. From the road we could see tiny little figures zigzagging down the hill and disappearing behind fir trees. We were anxious to join them, but first we needed lodging.

The first hotel turned us down, saying they had sufficient staff, but gave us the name of another place nearby. We could hardly contain ourselves when the manager of the second place said they happened to be short-handed, and hired us for the weekend. The manager said that we would be free to ski during the day in between serving breakfast and dinner, plus cleaning up the dining room. In return, we would get our meals and sleep in the bunkroom downstairs. Since it was getting late, we threw our bags on an empty bed, rented some gear and headed for the lifts.

The slopes of Mt. Snow surpassed my expectations. The powdery snow yielded easily to the slightest nudge of my skis, making my rather novice attempts look almost graceful. Gliding and turning effortlessly, I felt glamorous in my sleek, black ski pants and pink ski jacket with matching knitted cap and gloves. Skiing on such silky smooth snow was like driving on a newly paved highway with no holes or bumps. I could have stayed for hours, but the dipping sun reminded me to hurry back to the lodge, don my apron and start setting up for dinner.

I saw Steve that first night. Also a college student, he was one of the helpers at the hotel, fetching supplies, replenishing firewood, and waxing guests' skis, with the same arrangement of work for room and board for the weekend. If his smile hadn't won me over at first glance, then his charm would have. His sensitive, blue eyes and kind manner enveloped me like a cozy fur stole. There was an instant connection, the kind where you feel like you've always known the person, but have always been looking for them at the same time. We talked effortlessly, laughed easily and trusted each other immediately.

After my dinner shift, Steve and I told each other our life stories – we were both in our early twenties - over a glass of wine in front of a quietly romantic fire late into the night. I was smitten and he must have been, too. When he walked me to my bunkroom door and said he looked forward to seeing me the next day, he gave me a tender kiss. I had little need for sleep that night, preferring to relive the thrill of his lips on mine.

The following day, I could hardly concentrate on serving breakfast because my eyes kept wandering all over the lodge, trying to find Steve. Even after I finished work, I lingered around the dining room, hoping to see him before I went out to ski. Suddenly, he rushed up to me, flush-faced and out of breath, and said he was glad I hadn't left for the slopes yet. He had been hurrying with his chores so he could take a few hours off and we could ski together. I was overjoyed at my good luck. Shirley was busy anyway, flirting with a guy who worked in the kitchen.

We were having a magical time skiing when the sunlight started to wane, and we had to get back to the lodge. On the way back, Steve asked me to stop at another hotel in order to introduce me to his buddies, who were working there. They had all driven up from college together in a friend's car. Apparently Steve had told them about me and they wanted to see this woman their friend was raving about. I felt flattered and uncharacteristically shy, but pleased to meet them. I wondered how we might continue our relationship long distance after this weekend and felt sad that it might not be possible. After all, he was from New England, about 1,000 miles away from me and I was afraid that the old adage, "out of sight, out of mind," could describe our fate. Like me, he went to school full time and worked part time jobs. How would we find the time and money to travel to see each other?

Nevertheless, I was eager to spend as much time with him as possible, regardless of the outcome. We made plans to go out for drinks after work that evening. I wasn't used to drinking much, maybe a beer, at most two, with pizza every now and then, but lately I had been experimenting with mixed drinks like gin and tonic, vodka and orange juice and scotch and soda, to discover the world of hard liquor. I wanted to be savvy about names and ingredients of drinks like Manhattan, Martini and Whiskey Sour, so that I could sound worldly. I have no idea what I drank that night; I'm sure it wasn't much but, coupled with my state of infatuation with Steve, it made me tipsy. He was feeling no pain, as well. On the way home from the bar, he asked me to pull over and we fell into each other's arms, passionately kissing.

It was a clear, crisply cold night in which time stood still. There was nothing but the two of us and warm breath, moist tongues and fevered hands caressing every curve and muscle with our bodies wrapped so tightly that we moved as one. We were lying across the front seat with the motor still running for heat that turned out to be unnecessary. His features looked dreamy in the moonlight. Our legs and arms maneuvered deftly around the steering wheel and the gearshift. The windows were fogged up like a pale cocoon protecting us from the frost outside. I'll never know how belts and panties escaped from our closeness, or how we wound around each other to make love, but it was the most wonderful feeling I had ever had.

Waves of pleasure began to roll all over my body, slowly at first, then faster and more intense as I clutched him desperately inside me. I was nothing but a bundle of erotic sensations. My rational mind had ceased to exist. I felt safe, locked in his arms, pushing against him, breathing heavily. I could not have stopped even if I had wanted to. I had become helpless, completely merged with the orgasmic spasms that overcame me like a sparkling tide of bliss. I wanted this ecstasy to last forever. After a while, the ripples of delight began to subside, leaving me breathless and aglow. Only the warmth of his skin remained. Never before had I felt such rapture. Although I had enjoyed sex before, I now realized what I had been missing.

Gradually, we became aware of our surroundings and knew it was time to go. Reluctantly, we disentangled ourselves and got ready to return to the real world. The night with him had felt like a reverie. This time, our goodnight kiss at my bunkroom was passionate, almost desperate. We knew that time was running out and going to bed would mean waking up to face our last day at the lodge before heading home.

Indeed, the next day was busy with finishing work and packing, leaving little time for Steve and me to talk to each other. When I saw him, I felt somewhat embarrassed about my behavior the night before, but happy and even a bit smug about what I had discovered. We grinned and nodded knowingly. With everyone's suitcases, skis and other weekend trappings crowding the hallway, we said good-bye with no privacy in front of others, promising to keep in touch.

We wrote a few times about how we enjoyed meeting each other, but there was no basis beyond that to keep writing. Before long, classes, work and campus life got busy and our contacts petered out. If we had lived closer to each other, I think we might have pursued a relationship, but it wasn't meant to be.

I have rarely experienced such a thrilling night with another person as I had with Steve. It was unlike me to rush into romance with someone I had just met, but a number of factors of that frenzied weekend converged to transform me. First of all, I was looking for adventure, but I assumed that adventure would be the thrill of skiing on a beautiful mountain in a new place. And the skiing was fantastic, better than anywhere else I had been, but it was trumped by another, totally unexpected experience with Steve, that I would remember all my life.

Secondly, the setting of the lodge for a romantic tryst was too enticing to resist. Majestic, rough-hewn beams supported the rustic ceiling of fresh smelling cedar that perfumed the air. Huge picture windows looked out over pine forests framed by snow-covered peaks and punctuated with ski runs. The grand, yet earthy atmosphere was expansive and welcoming. It freed me of the constraints of the rule-bound dorm life back home.

Last but not least, my strong attraction to Steve, combined with a few drinks and opportunity, unfurled a sweet abandon within me. I was like a flower bud waiting for the right bee to unleash my nectar. Steve was gentle, yet firm, slow moving and intuitive, all the things I needed to feel relaxed and open.

Over the years, I've thought about Steve and wondered how he is. I hope he is happily married and having a good life. If we met up again, I doubt we would even recognize each other. And what if he's a hard-core Republican, or a religious fanatic, or has serious financial problems? Any of these elements could spell barriers to a relationship now that had no bearing on our feelings for each other that magical night. What a paradox to be able to feel so close to someone you've known only a short while, then possibly feel threatened by that same person as you learn more about their lifestyle and beliefs.

I guess in our innocence and yearning, we initially project only those qualities that we most want to see onto the blank screen of another person's life. But when reality sets in, they are altered or replaced by the person's real characteristics, which we may not like as much. Although the beginning stage of infatuation can't endure, it is a necessary and wonderful illusion upon which to build. In Steve, I really liked what I saw from the start and would gladly have risked discovering his other layers, if only fate had allowed.

Phone Calls

*   *   *

INEVER FOUND OUT FOR SURE how the man had gotten my phone number. I shared an apartment with another college student, but she was away for spring break. The first time he called I thought it was a wrong number. "Hello, hello? Is anybody there?" All I heard on the other end of the line was silence, then barely noticeable breathing. I found this mildly curious, but simply hung up and paid no further attention. When it happened again later that same day, I thought it could be a friend of mine playing a joke on me, and said "Come on, who is this?" Still no response, just silence and breathing. Who would keep calling me and not say anything? This time when I hung up, my stomach felt slightly queasy.

The thought that this wasn't a random mistake scared me. I hoped in vain that the calls would stop. When the phone rang again, I was afraid to answer it, yet intrigued by this mystery. "Hello, hello?" Again, silence. That evening when another call came, I felt more aggravated than nervous. I mustered up my strongest voice and demanded: "Stop harassing me! Don't call here again." Suspicious of every new sound, I slept fitfully that night alone in the apartment. When the calls continued the next day, I decided to call the police.

The policeman came over that afternoon, after I had received several more of the unsettling calls. He explained that, although I still had not heard the caller's voice at that point, it was most likely a man who called random numbers until he found a female at home. He presumed that the man liked the sound of my voice and enjoyed hearing my agitation when I got upset with him. Having this effect on me would give him a sense of power and importance. The officer said that men who do this tend to be lonely people with psychiatric problems, socially isolated, and usually harmless. He guessed the man was only seeking attention. I found the policeman's words somewhat comforting and started to breathe more easily. But I wanted to know how to put a stop to these calls.

The officer shocked me when he suggested the following: The next time the man called, instead of hanging up, I should try to stay on the line with him and engage him in conversation for at least half an hour, to give the police time to trace the call. My mouth must have dropped open as I gasped audibly, prompting the policeman to reassure me: "Miss, we'll have everything set up ahead of time and we'll work as fast as we can to try to locate the phone from which the man is making the calls. If he's using his home phone, we might be able to catch him and get him the help he needs." My initial hesitation eased when I heard that the man would potentially be helped with whatever problems he had. Plus, I was enticed by the adventure of it all. At age 22, I had never done anything as remotely exciting in my life. I agreed to do it.

That evening, when the phone rang again, my hand shook as I picked up the receiver. I tried to steady my voice and sound friendly: "Hello, you're the person who has been calling me. Are you lonely? Do you want someone to talk to?" After a brief pause, a low, gravelly voice responded: "Yes, I want to talk to you." My pulse was pounding in my throat as I heard myself ask him what he'd like to talk about. "Tell me what you are wearing," he said. I described the clothing I had on, but he wanted to focus only on certain things. "What kind of stockings are you wearing?" he asked. He probed in detail as to the material, color and style of my pantyhose. Then, "Are you wearing high heels?" He wanted me to describe my shoes, including the shape and height of the heels. I tried to sound as normal as possible, as I answered his strange questions. At the same time, I was anxiously watching the clock, wondering if the police were tracing the call. The man had me repeat the descriptions of my stockings and shoes over and over again. It was evident that he was mentally ill and I felt a bit sorry for him. After what I thought must have been half an hour, I said I had to go, hoping the police had had sufficient time.

As soon as we hung up, with my adrenaline still racing, I called the direct line the policeman had given me. He said they had traced the call, unfortunately not to a residence, but to a pay phone in a mall nearby, and it would be impossible to find the man that way. He thought it had been worth a try and praised me for the good job I had done by keeping him on the phone. After all that effort, I was disappointed, but also relieved that the ordeal was over. As I was about to end the call, the officer said, "There is one more thing we could try, if you are willing."

Part of me wanted nothing more to do with the caller, but I was curious to hear about the new suggestion. The next time a call came in, the policeman explained, I was to engage the man in conversation, claim to be interested in him, and finally suggest meeting him somewhere on the mall parking lot. The policeman would wait in plain clothes in an unmarked car, well away from our proposed meeting place, ready to make an arrest when the man approached me. I was not to get out of the car, and only roll the window down part way.

When he finished, I was already shaking my head and practically holding my breath, unable to imagine myself doing what he requested. But then he added, "I know it's a lot to ask, but you'd be doing a good service for the community if you would help us catch this guy." That last part cinched it for me. I was a pushover when my heroic nature was aroused, plus the outrageousness of the venture appealed to me, I had to admit.

The policeman said that the man might not show up at all, as was often the case with these men, because he most likely didn't want a real live encounter. Or, he might plan to come and then loose his courage. Or, he might actually come and see me from a distance, but stay hidden. The individuals varied, but most of them were content to stay in their fantasies, where they were in control and felt safe. We agreed that I would wait at the lot for half an hour, and leave if the man hadn't come by then.

When the phone rang again, I was prepared. I had rehearsed my spiel as planned, almost convincing myself that I wanted to meet him. To be honest, I did want to see what he looked like. After hearing my proposal, the caller hesitated at first, but when I promised to wear sheer stockings and high heels, he agreed. We set a day and time to meet on the far corner of the mall. When I informed the policeman of the date, he thanked me again for my cooperation and said that he would be there, but would stay out of sight of the man and me. He reiterated that most people making harassing calls with sexual innuendo are almost always non-violent, but he would protect me if necessary.

On the appointed day, I grabbed my purse with trembling hands and drove over to the mall. On the way, I wondered why on earth I had agreed to do this. Had I let my craving for adventure override my good judgment? But it was too late to back out now. I had given my word and the policeman would be expecting me.

With my heart in my throat, I pulled into the parking lot and left the motor running. There were a few other cars parked on the opposite side of the lot, but they seemed to be empty. I looked all around for movement in the bushes or the neighboring streets, but didn't see anybody. I wondered where the policeman was hiding. I sat on the edge of my seat for what seemed like forever, but the man didn't come. After waiting for almost an hour, I left.

In a way, I felt relieved that the caller had not shown up, at least as far as I knew. But I also felt disappointed. I had wanted to meet the man, look him in the eye and see what kind of person he was. I had always been interested in what makes people tick and this time was no different.

Shortly after I got home, the policeman called me and said he wasn't surprised that the man didn't show and thanked me again for my courage. He said he had been with me the whole time, but out of sight. I asked if he knew what caused this kind of mental illness, but he didn't. He said that the phone calls with most of the men – and all of the offenders were men - seemed to be cyclical, according to the phases of the moon, with a noticeable jump in calls at full moon. He didn't know what their diagnosis was, but guessed it was some sort of obsession. He said he doubted that the man would bother me again and, sure enough, I never got another call from him. But for weeks, my heart jumped every time the phone rang.

When it was all over, I couldn't believe I had participated in a police trap, and I was sure I didn't want to do anything like that again. It was too nerve-wracking. Although I was able to manage this one, intense occasion, which had been planned out and supervised by the police, I was not cut out for frequent, high-drama events. I would surely develop a stomach ulcer in very short order.

The experience did, however, pique my interest in mental illness. I wanted to know more about what causes such aberrations in human behavior and what could cure them. It was confusing that the man was articulate and sounded fairly normal, except for his fixation. I wondered if he had been born with this problem or had acquired it some other way. My curiosity wasn't strong enough at the time to push me to do any research on mental illness, but it would be one day, after I had had my own personal breakdown.

Rolfa and Herbert Wiesbauer
Augsburg, Germany

La Boheme

*   *   *

AFTER FINISHING MY MASTER'S DEGREE in German and Comparative Literature in 1964, I moved to Germany to become more fluent in the language. As part of a program through the German Embassy in Washington, DC, I received a stipend to teach English in German high schools in Augsburg, a city about an hour's drive northwest of Munich.

Looking for a room to rent, I placed an ad in the local newspaper and got three responses. One was a stark room on the fourth floor of an old building with no elevator. The other looked friendlier, but had a small coal stove for heat, for which I would have to haul the coal from the basement. Generally speaking, Germany had done a great job rebuilding the country after the Second World War, but not everyone had the means to modernize their properties. Still, I was used to certain creature comforts and felt disheartened as I headed to the third possible rental.

When we entered the neighborhood – one of the teachers had offered to drive me around to look for a place – my heart skipped a beat. Here were beautifully landscaped homes on quiet streets, similar to an American, middle class suburb. After we parked in front of the ivy-covered entrance, my step quickened and I hurried to ring the doorbell. As soon as Rolfa opened the door with her warm smile and sparkling eyes, I was smitten with her. She welcomed us inside and showed me the room that was for rent. It was spacious and nicely furnished, but I didn't want to show my excitement right away. On the phone, she had asked for 140 German marks per month, which was a bit above my budget. When I asked her if she would take 120 marks, she said yes without hesitating. She later told me she liked me right away, too, and really hoped I would take the room.

Rolfa told me that she and her husband Herbert liked renting rooms to students, especially English-speaking ones, in order to keep up their English skills. They had travelled widely, were well read, and enjoyed meeting interesting people from other cultures. To top it off, the Wiesbauers had two daughters, Uki and Uschi, who were close to my age of twenty-four years. Before long, we became friends, but I didn't see much of them, because they were both away at college and came home only on some weekends. However, Rolfa and I became close. Although she was twenty-five years older, she was like a big sister to me. Herbert was a civil engineer and had done well for himself after the war, especially after his company won a big contract with the occupying Americans to construct new buildings. I was invited to join them a few times on visits to their lake house near Munich and mountain house in Austria.

Rolfa and Herbert were frequent operagoers. When I told them I had never been to an opera, they offered to take me with them to Vienna to the National Opera House, where Puccini's famous romantic opera, "La Boheme," was playing. Herbert was born in Austria and had relatives there where we could stay. I couldn't wait to see my first opera. They had reserved tickets for themselves months in advance to be assured good seats, but had no extra ticket for me. I had to take my chances on getting one after we arrived. I hoped the money I had brought would be sufficient for a reasonably good seat. Even back then, opera was expensive, especially a popular Puccini opera. As a guest teacher, I wasn't earning much money, but at least I wouldn't have to pay for lodging.

Herbert drove the 250 miles from Augsburg to Vienna, most of the way on the autobahn, which had no speed limit. I was scared sitting in the back seat while Herbert averaged about 90 mph, the typical speed of many German drivers on the highway. As an American, with our conservative speed limits and our attention to safety, I was clutching the edge of my seat most of the way. I tried not to look out the front window, but concentrated on the rolling hills with their tiny chapels and grazing cows. Still, my mind recalled the bloody tangle of body parts and mangled metal I had often seen on German traffic reports on television. Sometimes at social gatherings when I would point out that the mortality rate on German highways was twice as high as in the U.S., people didn't seem to believe me. Incredibly, some of them even claimed that a lower speed limit would cause drivers to get bored, lose concentration, and cause more accidents! No amount of reasoning or statistical evidence could convince them otherwise.

As we neared the city and Herbert had to slow down, I breathed more easily, and my excitement grew. After we greeted Herbert's aunt and dropped our bags, we walked around downtown, since we had some time before the box office would open and I could get a ticket.

Vienna was the most charming of all the cities I had visited in my 24 years. Until this trip, I had only seen pictures of her magnificent beauty. In person, she didn't disappoint: century-old coffee houses, intricately carved building facades, and delicately woven wrought iron fences decorated the streets. The town seemed abloom with colorful flower stands on the street corners, antique carriages drawn by horses adorned with blossoms, and flower boxes gracing the windows. Classical music wafted from windows and competed with calls from vendors selling tantalizing sausages, huge pretzels, and chocolate candies wrapped in foil graced by Mozart's bust. The vitality of the place was contagious.

It was easy to fall in love with Vienna's old world flair. We admired quaint courtyards with rose gardens, and life-size sculptures from ancient Greek mythology as we strolled around. In a special craft store I bought my mother a purse with the well-known cross-stitch embroidery. The shopkeepers continued the old tradition of greeting customers like royalty: "Good day, my Lady," they would sing out, and bow with a flourish. In the theater district we spotted men dressed up in the attire from Mozart's time: skirted jackets, flouncy neckwear, tight knee stockings, and long, white ponytail wigs.

When the box office opened, I was disappointed to learn that that evening's performance of "La Boheme" was sold out – there were no seats left. When the cashier saw my unhappy face, he said: "But Miss, if you are a student, you can get standing room at the top of the theater, if there is any left." He directed me to the back of the theater, where, after waiting in a long line with other young people, I was ecstatic to obtain a standing room ticket. I was surprised that it only cost fifty cents, but happy that I would be able to see the opera after all.

That evening, my friends and I arrived early for the show so I would have time to see the plush, ornate interior of the building. The lobby was dazzling with its gilded statues, scarlet carpets and crystal chandeliers. The attendees walked arm-in-arm in a large circle around the room, as was their custom before the performance and during intermission. It was an ingenious way to greet acquaintances, to observe everyone's finery, and to stretch one's legs.

When the warning bells rang, we separated, my friends going to their seats, and I beginning my ascent into the heavenly realms of the top tiers. The climb was steep, and I soon saw why. The stairs ended at the very top of the theater, right beneath the dome-like ceiling, where, on either side of the stage, were rows of leaning bars, from which to watch the performance. The bars were sturdy, velvet-covered supports perched at the edge of a three-story drop to the orchestra pit. My heart lurched as I took my place, grasping the bar for dear life. The air was musty. I was fighting a claustrophobic feeling and I began to perspire, wondering if anyone had ever fallen from there.

As the music began and the curtain rose, however, I forgot my discomfort and focused on the performance. The richness of the instruments and the singers' voices captivated me. From my perch I could see only one third of the stage, and I couldn't understand the Italian, but it didn't matter. The emotional singing and gestures converged to tell the story of the artist's dying lover so passionately that it moved my soul, and became one of the most memorable experiences of my life. I've seen that opera in other venues since then, but nothing can compare with that first time. Of all the operas I've seen, "La Boheme" will remain my favorite.

Part of this special memory has to do with the Wiesbauers taking me there. Aside from Herbert's wild driving, I felt comfortable in their company on trips and in their home, where I lived for a year. Rolfa, especially, was generous with her time, explaining words and helping me improve my German. She had taught kindergarten briefly before marriage and was a patient teacher. In return, I gave sessions of English conversation to her and Herbert around their kitchen table. We had fun laughing at each other's mistakes, and developed a close friendship that lasted fifty years.

If more than two or three years passed without a visit to see them, I joked about needing a Wiesbauer "fix." In their old age, they were able to stay in their home with the help of their daughters and a live-in couple. Herbert was very confused and forgetful towards the end, and died at the age of 99. Rolfa remained alert and still wrote letters to me in her own beautiful handwriting until a few months before her death at the age of 100. She had even learned how to e-mail in her early nineties.

The Wiesbauers were so much a part of my life, in spite of the physical distance between us, that it's hard to adjust to a world without them. They always treated me like a member of the family, playfully calling me their third daughter. I could show up at their house any time and stay as long as I liked, as could any of their good friends. If anyone has ever loved me unconditionally in life, aside from my parents, it has been Rolfa.

Herbert and Rolfa were homebound for the last years of their lives, but they watched opera on television whenever they could. I was content to watch with them when I was there. Nowadays, I don't go to the theater often, but I can't see or hear anything about opera, especially "La Boheme," or Vienna, without a rush of nostalgia coming over me.

Neuschwanstein Castle
Hohenschwangau, Bavaria

Love at Neuschwanstein

*   *   *

ONE EVENING IN 1964, WHEN I was living in Augsburg, Germany, I went to a local, popular inn for supper after Italian class, which I was taking at the adult night school. The place was reasonably priced, an important consideration for me, since I was earning only a small stipendium teaching English at two high schools in the town. The inn was crowded, but there were a few empty seats at one of the large wooden tables. I asked the other patrons if I could sit down with them, since sharing tables was a common practice in less fancy restaurants in Bavaria. With my best German, I ordered a typical, light supper of sausage with potato salad.

In my effort to pronounce the German words correctly, I had not yet noticed who was sitting at the table, but one of the young men had noticed me. Peter heard my American accent and started to talk to me. He was good looking, and friendly, which helped me feel at ease. I was attracted to his soft, blue eyes and his sensitive voice. I noticed that he had a slight, nervous tic, which I found endearing – he would sometimes squeeze his left arm lightly into his left side. His fluent English, spoken with a charming, European accent, made him sound intelligent and cultured. When he told me about his internship as an accountant in food marketing in the U.S., I was flabbergasted to hear that he had lived in Takoma Park, Maryland, not far from where I lived in College Park. We knew all the same shops and cafes, which created an immediate closeness between us. I felt comfortable with him. Peter bought me a drink and we spent the evening talking.

Peter told me about a funny incident that happened to him one morning during the early 60's in Takoma Park. He was on his way to work at the nearby grocery store where he was learning the business. It was 6:00 a.m. and Peter was responsible for opening the store that day. Since he didn't have a car, he often went places on foot in the U.S., just as he did at home in Germany. That morning he was walking along the street, actually in the street, since there were no sidewalks in that area then, when a police cruiser pulled up beside him. The policeman got out and asked Peter for identification, then grilled him about where he was going and why. When Peter had answered all the questions satisfactorily, he asked the policeman why he had stopped him. The officer said that Peter had looked suspicious because he was walking, and most Americans don't walk...they drive everywhere in their cars!

Peter and I started to date, taking walks in the park or going out to dinner. My landlady Rolfa commented on my excited state whenever Peter was coming to pick me up. Indeed, my stomach would do flip-flops and I'd have a silly grin on my face. When he held my coat, opened the door for me, or poured my wine, he made me feel like a princess. One night, he took me to a dance at the "Hotel Drei Mohren," a fancy place with excellent food. He was graceful on his feet and held me at a proper gentleman's arm's length for our first dance, a heavenly waltz. But when the next song came on, a romantic one, called "Strangers in the Night," he pulled me in close and thrilled me with our first kiss. I still get teary eyed when I hear that song.

If all that wasn't enough to make me crazy about him, the clincher came the day we went to the fairy-tale-like castle, called Neuschwanstein, in southern Bavaria at the foot of the Alps. It was a sunny, late October day with a slight nip in the air when we set out to drive the two hours south of Augsburg. After we parked the car, we rode in an old-timey, open carriage, drawn by a team of two sleek horses up the steep hill towards the castle. As the horses carried us higher and higher, a dreamy mist hovered over the autumn foliage of burnt orange and wine reds. The horses snorted and blew as they pulled us farther up the windy road, their large jingle bells ringing merrily in step with their trotting hooves. The air was chillier now, the higher we went, and we were happy to snuggle under the warm blankets the driver had given us. Around the next bend, a light snow began to fall, powdering us like the top of a sugar cake. I never wanted this magical ride with Peter to end.

Touring the castle, we delighted in hearing the stories of wild King Ludwig, who had had the palace built. Since it was late in the season, we were in a small group of tourists, making the visit seem more personal. As we went room to gilded room, sumptuous with tapestries and sculptures, I fantasized about living there happily ever after with Peter, or anywhere, for that matter. We were married the following year. Although we didn't live in a castle, our rented duplex felt just as wonderful to me.

Part Three
Culture Shock

*   *   *

Our Wedding Day
1-29-1966

Early Years of Marriage

*   *   *

THE FIRST YEARS OF MARRIAGE with Peter in Augsburg were exciting and challenging. The beautiful, old city was familiar to me from having rented a room there with Rolfa and Herbert when Peter and I started dating. In preparation of my arrival as his wife, Peter had rented a duplex for us at 4 Malmedystrasse and had made some renovations, like painting and carpeting the stairs. I liked the place immediately, especially the quaint cement pond with its cherub fountain on the patio out back. I hoped frequent guests would inhabit the extra room upstairs. I was still in touch with Rolfa and Herbert, who had moved to the next village by then, but I wanted to meet some couples our age. I scoped out the neighborhood, not only to find the nearest butcher and baker, but also to meet people that might become friends.

To my disappointment, it was nearly impossible to make friends during the course of running errands. People were focused on the task at hand, neither offering nor inviting chit-chat. Most of our neighbors seemed to value their privacy as symbolized by fences or hedges in front of their houses, as if to mark their territory. Oftentimes, you had to ring the doorbell at a gate, gaining access to the front door only if buzzed into the front yard by the occupant.

Peter worked as marketing manager at a super market chain called BMA (Bernard Mueller, Inc.). At first, his hours were ideal for us newlyweds. After working 9 a.m. to 5 p.m. on Monday through Wednesday, he got off at 4 p.m. on Thursdays and at 3:30 p.m. on Fridays, which gave us plenty of time to go on outings in the afternoons and evenings before dark. Weather permitting, we'd sit on the patio first for coffee and cake, a 4:00 o'clock tradition all across Germany, then take long walks or ride our bikes on the nearby trails until dark, often ending up at a restaurant for a meal.

In summer we'd take off for the pool or the lake for a swim before dinner. I had to get used to swimming in the frigid water, since the outside air rarely reached the upper 70's, not hot enough to heat the water to a comfortable temperature. After swimming, I sat shivering in a wet suit, in spite of a fluffy towel and Peter's arm around my shoulders. I missed lounging in the warm sun after a dip.

One day, while sitting on the sandy shore of the lake we frequented, I saw a woman standing with a large beach towel around her. She clutched both ends of the towel in one hand and began to squirm around underneath it. I was shocked when Peter explained that she was changing out of her wet bathing suit. Sure enough, seconds later, her wet suit plopped onto the ground. Then, after a bit more wriggling, she stepped away from the towel in a dry suit. I wondered how she could so deftly pull down the wet suit and pull up the dry one while holding the towel around herself, not revealing her nakedness. I'd never seen anyone do that before.

Peter said that Germans considered it unhealthy to sit in the chilly air in a wet suit and there weren't always facilities available for changing. He also said that Europeans were generally less modest than Americans, but that I should just discreetly look away. As a child I had always hated sitting in a wet suit after swimming and had often felt itchy on my bottom. I wanted to try it, too.

On my first attempt, I got my feet all tangled up in the towel and dropped the corners of it, exposing my backside, but I kept practicing every time we went swimming. Finally, I got the hang of it and could change into a dry suit, pleased as punch with myself. To this day, I change out of my wet suit in public, no matter where I am, even though Americans might consider the practice highly irregular, if not downright inappropriate, if they knew what I was doing.

On the other side of our duplex lived a nice, though quite reserved lady with her husband who often travelled on business. A tall, attractive woman, she was around fifty, close to twice my age, and either introverted or depressed. I couldn't tell which. When we met on the street, she would smile slightly, nodding only a quick "Guten Tag" and disappear into her house. More than once, I wanted to go next door and have coffee with her for company, but was afraid to bother her. I had been feeling lonely during the day and found myself counting the hours until Peter got home from work.

One early spring day after we had lived there about six months, she invited me to accompany her to the nursery where she bought blue phlox every year to plant on her front stoop. She wanted me to buy the same flowers to plant on my stoop, so the two sides would match. I was very excited at the prospect of going somewhere with someone and could hardly wait for the appointed time. My neighbor helped me choose the young flowers, which came in small containers ready to plant, and showed me how to plant them so they would thrive.

Growing up, I was used to planting seeds directly into the ground, but Germany's colder climate was too harsh to support tiny seedlings. They needed a head start in a protective green house. After our pleasant outing, I hoped my neighbor and I would become friends, but she went back to keeping mostly to herself. Still, every year in spring I think of her when I pick out the bedding plants for my garden and I try to make sure blue phlox are among them.

In the early years, Peter and I took a few short trips together. I wanted to rent a camper and just take off exploring different places, but he had never been camping before and wanted the creature comforts of hotels, which required planning and scheduling ahead. There were very few hotels and motels along the road, making spontaneous travel difficult. To be assured of a room almost anywhere, prior reservations were necessary. Although Germany's rebuilding efforts after the war were truly miraculous, accommodations were still scant in many areas.

Once, we tried to go skiing at a small resort in Austria, called Hintertux, a quaint village tucked away at the foot of some tall mountains, literally at the dead end of one of those narrow, curvy mountain roads, which had already made me nervous on the drive there. After renting our equipment, we set out for the chair lift on the first day. Without a second thought, I climbed into the chair lift, which was single, not double. I had always disliked chairlifts, but could manage going with someone on a double chairlift without feeling too scared. This time, I thought I could handle the ride alone as long as Peter was close by. Thankfully, he got into the one behind me about forty feet away, but as soon as my feet left the ground, I knew I was in trouble.

The familiar signs of a panic attack – the pounding heart and difficulty breathing - came on quickly. Since I knew from experience that talking to someone could help control my anxiety, I tried to call to Peter behind me, but from the distance, he couldn't hear what I was saying and didn't understand what was wrong. To make matters worse, as we ascended, the chair's altitude got higher and higher from the ground. Other chair lifts I had taken stayed fairly close to the ground, but this one was already above the pine trees with no end station in sight. It was the longest lift ride I had ever taken. I felt trapped and my panic became full blown, to the point where I felt like I was suffocating, or having a heart attack, or both. When we reached the top, I felt relieved, but wanted to go back down on the next lift right away, much to Peter's dismay. He took it in good grace, but it's hard for anyone who has never experienced a panic attack to really understand what it is like. I wish I had sought help with a therapist back then to find out the reasons for my anxiety and to learn to manage it better.

We undertook another outing when I was about six months pregnant with Chris, also involving heights. In order to reach a popular lunch destination on a particular mountain in Bavaria, we had to take a gondola ride for about ten minutes. After the Hintertux debacle, I was a bit hesitant, but felt brave enough to do it. After all, the gondola was a sturdy, metal capsule roomy enough to hold a dozen people. Since I also had the tendency towards claustrophobia in cramped spaces, I talked to Peter and our fellow passengers during the ascent to keep my mind occupied and my anxiety under control.

Not long into the trip up the mountain, I began to feel mild stomach cramps, which became worse the higher we went. I knew it wasn't panic I was experiencing, because I'd never had abdominal pain with panic, but I had no idea what it was. I told Peter, who tried to reassure me by saying we would be at the top soon. But by the time we arrived and stepped out of the gondola, the cramps were almost unbearable, causing me to double over in pain. We had no choice but to take the next gondola back down, in the hopes of finding a doctor at the bottom. The closer we got to the ground, the more my pains abated until, finally, they disappeared altogether. Thankfully, once on the ground, I was back to normal, although still shaky, but our trip had been ruined.

My gynecologist later told me that the high altitude with its thinner air had most likely caused the cramping because I was pregnant. She said we were wise to have come back down the mountain right away. If we had stayed up there longer, the baby might have been damaged or I might have even miscarried. As it was, no harm had been done. From then on, I shied away from heights until the baby was born, except to admire them from the ground.

I often felt isolated while Peter was at work. Back home in the U.S., I was used to being active and among people. Luckily, I found a job teaching German classes to Americans at the local military bases in Augsburg, which helped me pass the time. I also taught one semester of German for the University of Maryland on an American base in Munich, commuting back and forth in my yellow Carman Ghia until my belly got too tight to fit behind the steering wheel. It was refreshing to be among Americans, where I could speak English and feel connected right away.

While teaching, I did meet some American couples to invite over to dinner a few times, but they often moved on to their next assignment, just as we were becoming friends. Since Peter was relatively new in his job, he didn't know many people yet and Germans tended to take longer to warm up to newcomers. Also, he was in a supervisory position, which generally discouraged socializing with employees in a lesser status.

Along with teaching for the military came privileges at the P.X. and the commissary, where I was able to buy American clothes and food, welcome items to help fight bouts of homesickness that flared up from time to time. Overall, however, I was adjusting fairly well, especially with the newfound avenues to be among my countrymen now and then. Life was fairly satisfying and Peter and I were getting along well most of the time.

Chris was born on May 19, 1967 in the hospital at the U.S. Army base on the outskirts of Augsburg, weighing in at 8 1/2 pounds, a large baby at that time. We fell in love with him immediately. He was pudgy and rosy-cheeked, as if someone had applied rouge to his face. Hard to imagine now-a-days, but pre-natal care and delivery were part of the benefits I had as a German teacher on the American military base.

Because of security regulations, no visitors except spouses were allowed on the maternity ward, but Peter's mother Gertrud wasn't going to let anyone stop her from seeing her first grandchild. She had waited a long time for this moment. So when no one was looking, she snuck up the back stairwell of the hospital and crept up to the window of the nursery, where she met Peter and me and stood staring at Chris, drinking in his infant beauty, if only for a few moments. Luckily, no one noticed her and she snuck back down the stairs, undetected. That was the first and last time I ever knew my mother-in-law to break any rules. She brought me a gorgeous gold pin in the shape of a round knot for producing her new grandson, and built and hand painted a magnificent cradle with flowers and woodland creatures for him. Unfortunately, it was destroyed in a basement flood years later. My father-in-law, Helmut, was equally excited about his grandson, but opted to wait until I was discharged with Chris before meeting him.

I loved being a mom, nursing and caring for Chris and pushing him in his baby carriage. We were a family now and I was feeling more at home in Augsburg. I had made a good friend, Heidi, across the street, the kind of friend where I felt comfortable showing up at her door unannounced to borrow a cup of sugar, a rarity during my time in Germany. Things were going smoothly for Peter at work. He was well respected and seemed happy, but another super market company from northern Germany made him an offer he couldn't refuse. It would be a big promotion with more responsibilities and challenges for him. With a sad heart but a feeling of excitement towards our new future, we said our good-byes to Augsburg, and headed for Bremen.

Helmut Eduard Spranger
(10-05-1901 to 1-17-1973)

and Benjamin Overstreet, Two Proud Grandfathers

Airing the Duvets

*   *   *

As a young housewife in Germany, I was trying to fit in and do things right. Some customs were very different, like eating the hot meal of the day at noon, and having open sandwiches for supper, but I tried to adhere to them for Peter's sake, since we were living in his country, and to be in sync with other people. Also, most stores shut down from one to three o'clock for an extended lunch hour and rest period, then closed for the day at six o'clock, such that I had to plan my time carefully to catch the shops open. Another inconvenience was that the washing machine took an hour and a half to do one load and most people did not have clothes dryers. Actually, I didn't mind hanging the clothes on a clothesline to dry, like my mother used to do. The fresh air gave them a pleasant, ozone smell.

One thing that really appealed to me was the German way of making beds with duvets, a much more efficient method than the unwieldy way I learned growing up. At home, my mother taught me to use a bottom sheet, a top sheet and a light or warm blanket, depending on the season, topped off by a bedspread and sometimes pillow shams. These multiple layers tended to conspire against me when I tried to line them up straight, fold the corners neatly and smooth the lumps. It took some time to make a bed neatly, American style. Whoever thought up this awkward procedure must have had a lot of time on their hands. No wonder American kids balk at making their beds.

Making the bed in Germany, on the other hand, was an easy task. You simply grabbed the end of the duvet at the bottom of the bed and shook it as hard as you could. The only real trick was to allow it to float down on top of the mattress as evenly as possible, so as not to make wrinkles. After a bit of practice, this took about twelve seconds. Since the pillow was smaller, it was easier to fluff, but the principle was the same. You were basically re-aerating the goose feathers by shaking them to lift them back up from their smashed, slept-on state. This took about four seconds.

Germans didn't bother with bedspreads. Their duvet covers, which were like giant pillow cases buttoned on the bottom edge for easy removal, came in lovely linen or damask, in all colors and designs. Some had modern, abstract patterns; others had an antique flair, any style to fit your taste and décor.

In spite of their reputation for cleanliness, Germans drew the line when it came to laundering sheets. They weren't about to wrestle that duvet out of its cover more than once a month. At the two-week mark, they would turn the duvet and the pillow over and call that fresh enough. Of course, the flat bottom sheet could be changed easily as needed. Most people sent their sheets out for mangling, a kind of ironing done on a wide, hot roller covered with padding. Once I tried to iron a duvet cover at home by hand and almost flipped over the ironing board. It was so cumbersome that I could hardly keep from stepping on it, while being careful not to iron my hand.

Germans did air out their duvets, however, but they had rules about it, which I didn't know until my German neighbor fussed at me. She was a spunky, elderly lady who monitored our comings and goings from her window. She had already reminded my husband Peter and me to keep the widely observed quiet time between 1:00 and 3:00 p.m., because she liked to nap then. I knew from earlier visits to Germany that people don't phone each other, mow the lawn or let their kids outside during those two hours, because "someone could be resting."

One warm, sunny day in April, I decided to air out our duvets. I had finished hanging them over the balcony railing and had sat down with a cup of coffee, when the doorbell rang. It was my grey-haired neighbor, furrowing her brow.

"Frau Spranger, I just dropped by to tell you something you may not know."

"Oh, sure, please come in."

"I noticed you hanging your duvets over the railing, but you shouldn't do that today."

"Why not?" I ventured, "the weather's so nice."

"Oh, yes, but there's an 'r' in the month," she exclaimed.

"A what?" I asked, thinking I hadn't understood her German correctly.

"An 'r'. You know, the letter, 'r'. When there's an 'r' in the month, like from September through April, it's unhealthy to air out the duvets. You see, those months have dampness in the air, even if it's warm outside. You can get arthritis if dampness gets into the down feathers. Your neighbor on the other side has terrible arthritis and she used to air out her duvets all year. You don't want that to happen. It's safe to air them out from May 1st through August 31st, months without "r's.""

I said I hadn't realized that, thanked her for her kind words and ran upstairs to bring in the duvets. As I gathered them into my arms, I could see her standing in her yard, looking up at me. With a slight smile on her face, she nodded her head in approval. I quickly nodded back to her, and escaped inside. I held the duvets to my nose and drank in the intoxicating freshness. I would gladly have taken the risk of arthritis to continue hanging the duvets outside on sunny days in months with an 'r', but I was afraid to risk inciting the disapproval of my vigilant neighbor.

The Reeperbahn

*   *   *

MY HUSBAND PETER AND I had just enjoyed a delicious fish dinner with another couple at a popular restaurant along the wharf of an old section of Hamburg called the "Reeperbahn," when we decided to stroll around a bit. The area was traditionally known for its red light district, full of seedy bars with loud sailors and sleazy hotels that rented rooms by the hour. Local newspapers routinely reported street fights and drug busts. One of the largest city police stations was located there, but couldn't stop the crime. The public seemed to view these events as common for a port town, except when muggings ended in fatal stabbings or pimps murdered their girlfriends. Such tragic news, thankfully rare, dominated the headlines when it happened, causing an outcry for tighter security, but only for a few days. Soon the incident would be forgotten and things would go back to normal. Prostitution was legal in Germany, but it was difficult to safeguard the women, especially around a harbor with so many easy hideaways among the docks.

In spite of, or perhaps because of, its reputation, the "Reeperbahn" had always drawn inquisitive and brave tourists. The ambience of the area and its promise of adventure enhanced the attraction, especially for me as an American in my mid-twenties. I certainly knew of "ladies of the night," but had never seen any in person. Since prostitution was illegal in the towns where I grew up, business had to be conducted under cover; whereas in Germany, prostitutes practiced openly. They had to be licensed by the state, which required them to have regular, physical check-ups to confirm good health. I was newly married, living abroad for the first time and most curious to see their intriguing ways. By the time Peter and I visited, entrepreneurs were revitalizing the harbor area as a trend-setting destination, but it was still a mixture of shady and avant garde. When we left the restaurant close to midnight, we were all rather tipsy. We had imbibed a little too much of the wine that our waiter lauded as a perfect complement to our meal, and were sauntering happily down the street.

The nearby Elbe River emitted a strong, brackish odor, as low, mournful horns echoed from invisible flatboats making their way to the North Sea. Large cargo ships hunkered at the docks, their iron anchor chains menacing against the black water. We drew our wraps more tightly around our shoulders and quickly crossed the pavement. The light was brighter under the antique gas lamps, which cast a warm glow on the cobblestones.

Down the dark alleyways we could see blinking, neon arrows pointing to rickety stairways that led to shade-drawn windows. I could imagine what was generally taking place behind them, but wondered about the details. After a few minutes' walk, we stumbled upon a short, dead-end street. From a distance, we noticed rows of large, full-length picture windows in the front of buildings, revealing muted light from old fashioned, fringed lamps while the gaslights outside lent an eerie haze over the district. The entrance to the street was partially blocked off by a low wooden fence, as if to keep out those who had no business there.

Our curiosity piqued, we went closer and saw a slow stream of men entering and exiting the area, their caps drawn over their eyes. From the fence we could see the windows more clearly. On the stuffed sofas and armchairs were women dressed like colorful mannequins, posing voluptuously, as if on display for sale. And they were. For sale. I was stunned and rooted to the spot, struck by this raw and immediate view of prostitution. Scanty bodices plunged, exposing generous bosoms; tight dresses rode up promisingly. Enticing smiles were etched on their faces, embellished by poufy hair in garish hues of red, blond, purple and blue-black, such that the women seemed unreal. The scene was titillating and I couldn't stop staring.

Since my husband and friends, all Germans, had seen similar sights in other European cities, they were not shocked. They also knew not to stick around and attract attention. "Come on, Pat, we're not supposed to be here," my husband urged. I reluctantly followed him, even though I wanted to stay and see how the business was transacted. I had seen the men milling around in front of the windows and wanted to watch what they would do next.

Nearby corners teemed with hookers on foot. Prospective customers crept up slowly in cars, their headlights illuminating the women from head to toe. As if assigned to a specific spot, each woman paced up and down in her few square yards, while calling attention to her best features. Some women stretched a fish-netted leg forward while tracing it upwards with a long, pointy fingernail; others dipped and twisted their chests, while crooking their arm behind their head. They strutted like exotic birds, feigning indifference when a car passed them by. The red rouge and curled lashes did little to mask the vacant eyes and hard lines at the mouth.

Occasionally, a car would slow to a stop and a man's head would emerge from the dark interior to exchange a few words with one of the women. We could only see heads shaking no and the car continuing on, or heads nodding yes and the car stopping while the woman got in, an apparent deal having been struck. Our friend's wife and I joked with each other about how much we would charge for our services.

On one corner several prostitutes lined up close to each other, as if in a chorus line. They inadvertently slouched in sync, one hand on a hip, and faced away from us toward the oncoming cars. I found it humorous and giggled to our friends. I don't know what suddenly possessed me but I wanted to line up with them. Against my better judgment, the impulse took on a life of its own and carried me away from my group up to the curb next to the prostitute nearest me. She was still looking in the opposite direction when I attempted to copy her slouch, and propped my hand on my hip like hers, doing my best to look sexy.

I had not meant for the woman to see me. I was trying to be funny and show off for my husband and friends, who froze, not knowing what to do. Then Peter gasped and started towards me. In that moment, the woman turned and caught me imitating her. She glared at me, harrumphed loudly, then braced her shoulders and headed towards me. She was upon me so fast, I wasn't able to retreat. She got up in my face and bellowed: "You're not pretty enough to be one of us!" With that, she turned on her heel, stalked off, and resumed her post at the curb.

I was flabbergasted more than scared. By then Peter had his arms around me, pulling me to safety. His face was ashen as he chastised me for my behavior. "You shouldn't have done that. She could have beaten you up." He was right, and in a way she did beat me up. She struck back at me with an insult that packed a punch. I've always remembered what she said, and always wondered whether she really thought I wasn't pretty enough. She hit my vulnerability squarely in the face, because like most women, I wanted to be considered pretty.

Under normal circumstances, I would have been more sensitive to the possibility of offending the prostitute, but at the time this incident occurred, I was not thinking about how my actions might affect her feelings. In my slightly intoxicated state, I was simply being silly, in no way intending to ridicule or demean her. She could not have known this, of course, and reacted the only way she knew how, to defend herself by lashing out at me. She wouldn't have known that, when sober, I sympathized with the plight of women who find themselves in her situation, that I would gladly have helped her find a different path for herself, one that would have lent her the dignity that she truly deserved as a human being, not one that required her to be dominated by other people.

Getting to Nude

*   *   *

THERE I WAS, WITHOUT A stitch of clothing on me, strolling along the nudist beach among crowds of other nudists on the German island of Sylt in the North Sea. If someone had told me that I would one day be naked in public, the stuff of nightmares, I wouldn't have believed it. My husband Peter had taken me to Sylt the first summer after we got married to show me his favorite vacation place, a sea resort with wide, snowy white beaches. I was a 26-year-old American, who had only seen a few topless sunbathers on the French Riviera once, and in a secluded, designated area of a German swimming pool a few times. I had been tempted to take my top off and join them, but never found the courage.

I was raised around good, God-fearing Southern Baptists on my father's side, who probably would have condemned public nudity as indecent at the very least, demonic at the very worst. Some of my more devout relatives didn't even dance or play cards, and would have considered such activities akin to courting the devil and risking one's soul. My mother, however, not having been raised with any particular church affiliation beyond general Christian, disapproved of her in-laws' religious rigidity, calling it "narrow-minded." She enjoyed going to dances with my father at the Elks Club, and playing bridge with other couples. Yet in some ways, she was prudish, too. When she tried to answer my questions about sex, for example, she would lower her voice and glance over her shoulder to make sure no one else could hear us. When undressing, even in front of my sister and me, she would hold a towel loosely to her breast, upholding the required gesture of modesty.

The wife of one of my paternal uncles, Aunt Frances, had a more enlightened approach to the whole matter of nakedness, which appealed to me. She believed that our bodies were created by God, and therefore natural and good, certainly nothing to be ashamed of. It was at her house that I, as a young girl of six or seven, first witnessed a family undressing in front of each other, putting bathing suits on and taking them off, or getting in and out of the shower, making no attempt to hide themselves. Their naturalness appealed to me, and I wanted to feel just as relaxed about my own body. I also admired Aunt Frances for her outspokenness and wanted to emulate her when I grew up. She would have fit right in at the nudist beach on Sylt and she would have gotten a kick out of seeing all the different shapes and sizes moving freely about in the fresh air.

Like many other German beaches, there were two sections on Sylt: a so-called "textile" beach, for people in bathing suits, and a nudist beach, the two barely divided by a small stretch of empty sand. Peter had spent several vacations there in his youth and was comfortable on both sides of the beach. I had never seen a nudist beach and was dying to go there from the moment we arrived. A voyeuristic excitement tingled all over me as I tried to imagine what it would look like. Since our hotel was on the textile side of the beach, we had to wear our bathing suits along the shore to cross the bluff between the two beaches. Peter assured me that the nude bathers wouldn't mind us strolling along "their" shoreline. Many others clad in suits did the same, simply to extend their walk, or out of curiosity, or with the intention of eventually joining them. I was glad not to feel pressured to disrobe on the first day.

My normally vivid imagination had not prepared me for the sight of that large expanse of beach, teeming with naked bodies of all ages, heights and widths, in various states of activity as far as the eye could see. In some ways, it was just like any other beach on a hot, sunny day. People were splashing in the surf, walking along the shore, wading in the foamy swirls or just gazing out at the horizon. Some were glistening on blankets, oily with suntan lotion, or perhaps playing with a beach ball, or a shuttlecock and paddle. Curvaceous figures mixed among wrinkly, middle-aged pear shapes. Proud and trim muscles strutted alongside saggy, beer-fed bellies. Children were building their sand castles, rushing after small waves, shrieking from the shock of cold water. Young and old, tall and thin, short and fat, everyone was having a great time. And everything looked perfectly normal, except that they were naked!

In their amazement, my eyes jumped away from me, cartoon-like, and visited perfect strangers at close range, in intimate places. They darted in and out of the crowd like ill-mannered children, sneaking around without permission, defying the rules. A color wheel of pale to dark tan shades painted the view. The white skin of new arrivals threatened to burn, while leathery-dry skin spoke of years of sun adoration. I was devouring the body buffet, staring unabashedly, mesmerized.

There were whole families naked together picnicking, reading, snoozing, acting as if this were their everyday routine. They looked quite content, smiling and conversing naturally. I felt somewhat embarrassed and very confused at these unusual sights. One woman had only one nipple, her breast having been removed on one side. She was engrossed in a game, laughing and hitting a ball enthusiastically over a net. She seemed oblivious to her fading scar, as if she had now fully become this woman of one breast. One elderly, bearded man was meditating in a yoga pose at the edge of the water, standing on his head with his legs crossed. Some of his other body parts, although yielding properly to gravity, curiously appeared to be upside down. I marveled at the apparent ease with which the nudists moved around, unprotected from natural elements, intruding eyes and possible moralistic attack. They looked so happy.

I wanted to join them, to dare to expose myself and see what it felt like to experience the ultimate physical disclosure. That night, I decided not to let the Puritan Ethic hold me back and asked Peter to help me take the plunge. The first day, we chose a spot as far back on the nudist beach as possible, partially shielded by a dune. We undressed and I sat crouched and stiff, as if stuck to our towel on the ground, hoping no one could see me back there. What if someone I knew came along? I felt vaguely ashamed, but also proud of myself for facing a scary new adventure. Peter looked relaxed, having done this many times before. He was grinning at me, amused at my untypical self-consciousness. I liked the direct contact of air all around me, while the warm sunrays fingered my skin.

The second day, we moved our towels closer to the crowd, but still kept some distance. This time I stood up with my naked body, fighting the immediate impulse to cover myself with my hands. I gasped barely audibly, my voice sounding as shaky as my knees felt. The sandy breeze peppered mildly at my naked skin, titillating and pleasing me. I tried taking a few steps but I had never walked so unencumbered like this before with nothing to hold me together. The space around me was endless and threatened to pull me into streams of nothingness. My arms and legs had trouble coordinating themselves, angling clumsily in the open void, like disconnected parts of someone else. I clutched at my husband's arm for reassurance, feeling both timid and liberated at once.

When I first stood up, I had expected people to stare at me, but no one was paying any attention. No heads were turning my way. I was secretly disappointed, since showing the world my naked body seemed so outrageous an act to me. I had expected at least a few glances. Little by little, the crowd was pulling me into itself, lending me some of its easy bravura and soothing confidence. By afternoon, we had inched ahead, all the way to the water for a dip. I loved the feel of the salty sea directly on my naked skin, and allowed it to engulf me. I felt vulnerable, yet safe, but mostly vital and real, merging completely with nature for the first time.

On the third day, familiarity and resolve were beginning to take effect. My eyes had returned to their usual, well-mannered composure, no longer gawking at the other people. This time, I took my clothes off right in the middle of the beach, without so much as a towel within reach. I still felt some awkwardness, but could now walk normally with my feet securely connected to the ground. I had finally done it! After only three days of gradual steps, I was able to shed years of conditioning about covering myself with clothes around other people. I was one of them now, a new convert still, but I had passed all the required rites of the initiate. I was proud of myself for being so brave and overcoming a strong inhibition that had never made logical sense to me. I also felt rather smug with a new adventure story to write my American friends back home. After all, I was a European now, at least by marriage, and beginning to acquire some of the manners and sophistication befitting the continent.

This trip to the nudist beach had been an exhilarating struggle, shedding years of conditioning to a new, exciting acceptance of my body, as if I had broken a secret code to physical freedom. I would never view nudity with the same eyes again. If I returned to Sylt today after many years of living in the U.S., I wonder how it would feel to walk naked on the beach again. Could I regain the same sense of abandon that I experienced back then, or would I slip back into my old cultural inhibitions? Either way, I would love to try it again, but, at the very least, I'm sure it would take me the same three days to get all the way down to nude.

Encounters with German Food

*   *   *

ADJUSTING TO LIFE IN GERMANY with my husband Peter was challenging in many ways, especially when it came to food. After living with the Wiesbauer family for a year in Augsburg and eating out with Peter, I got used to some of the Bavarian-style cooking and had even grown to love some regional dishes, like liver dumpling soup, veal sausages with sauerkraut, and pork roast with red cabbage. But I still disliked the typical breaded and fried foods, like Wiener schnitzel, and butter sauces for vegetables, like creamed cauliflower. My mother had tried to avoid extra fat in her kitchen, believing it to "clog your arteries."

As a child, I had been very picky about food. I must have driven my parents crazy when I refused to eat many foods, particularly healthy ones. They made me sit at the dinner table for what seemed like hours, insisting that I eat my peas or squash, which I tried to hide under the table, stick into a plant, or feed to the dog. They meant well, I know, and worried that I was too skinny. I frequently caught colds. Eventually, they would get tired of waiting for me to finish my plate and would let me off the hook with one more bite.

As an adult, that gradually changed. I discovered that food was one of life's greatest pleasures and I began to eat most things with gusto, no longer a problem eater, or so I thought, until one time early in our marriage when Peter and I were out to eat and he ordered one of his favorite meals called "Beefsteak Tartar." I had heard of it but wasn't sure what it was. When it arrived, I couldn't believe my eyes. There was a huge pile of curly, raw ground beef, topped with chopped onion and a raw egg, looking to me like it all needed to be cooked. But Peter dug in enthusiastically, smacking his lips in delight. When he offered me a bite, I declined, which apparently annoyed him and led to one of our first arguments. He thought I should be willing to at least try everything, not understanding that the very sight of his dish turned my stomach. In fact, I didn't even want to kiss him that night.

My mind put this incident in the area of exception to the rule, so I still considered myself a cosmopolitan eater, until, that is, Peter changed jobs and we moved to northern Germany. We lived in a village called Leeste, outside of Bremen, which was a city situated west of Hamburg near the North Sea, where the cuisine was quite different. While there had been very little seafood in southern Germany, which was mostly inland and alpine, there was an abundance of it now, but unfamiliar varieties to me and fixed in ways I was unaccustomed to.

One day Peter took me out to eat at a nice seafood restaurant, where the waiter highly recommended the fish on special that day. I was quite hungry and eager to try a new fish. When it was served, however, my stomach became queasy. It was a whole fish, sprawled open-mouthed across a large plate, staring up at me through filmy, grey eyes. My husband seemed startled and the waiter somewhat indignant, when I sent the fish back to the kitchen to have its head removed. When the fish came out again, it was tasty enough, but by then I had lost most of my appetite.

Sometimes at buffet parties, food would surprisingly become an issue for me. The display of colors and textures would look enticing at first, but when I looked more closely and saw the smoked eel, roast tongue, venison, caviar or other unfamiliar delicacies, I often settled for Swiss cheese and crackers, again to the dismay of my husband. Even the shrimp was different and had a strange, fishy taste. They were tiny, hardly an inch long when peeled, not the big, plump ones I was used to on the east coast. An ice-cold shrimp cocktail served on a bed of lettuce in a pretty goblet had always been a favorite of mine back home.

Once, on New Year's Eve, Peter's aunt made a special herring salad for family and friends invited to her house for the festive occasion. The salad looked innocent enough, the chopped fish mixed in a creamy sauce with sliced apples and onions, served in a lovely pottery bowl. The family was excited about it, as this aunt's reputation for herring salad was legendary. I smiled with them and geared up to try it, hoping it might resemble tuna fish salad, which I loved.

All eyes were on me as everyone awaited my reaction. My feigned enthusiasm belied my taste buds as I chewed the first bite of herring. It had not been cooked, but only marinated in a vinegary solution with the onions, bay leaves and peppercorns. It had a strong flavor like bracken ocean water, but I did my best to eat some. I picked out some of the apples and onions to eat, and then spread the rest around the plate, hoping no one would notice that I wasn't eating much. I emptied my wine glass, which only half masked the fishy aftertaste, and ruined the good wine in the process.

Later that evening, after the New Year had been properly toasted with champagne, Peter's aunt brought out the main dish, an enormous boiled carp, which was a traditional holiday fish in some regions of Germany, thought to bring good luck. I wasn't feeling very lucky when I saw him. My eyes must have grown as wide as the carp's, and my mouth dropped down in bewilderment. Both the fish and I seemed to have been caught off guard, momentarily frozen in place, wishing to be elsewhere. Again, after a deep breath, I did my best to express admiration for the cook's creation and braced myself for another round of seafood.

This fish wasn't bad, as far as boiled fish goes, but the texture felt blubbery on my tongue. As a whole, the meal was a far cry from my mother's wonderful holiday fare, which always had a huge, golden brown turkey at its center, stuffed with a mouth watering sage dressing and surrounded by overflowing bowls of mashed potatoes, gravy, candied sweet potatoes, succotash, cranberry sauce and hot rolls. All my life, I had eaten these dishes at holiday time. Without them, it didn't feel like the holidays at all. I pasted a smile on my face, hoping to hide my disappointment. But even the ice cream we had for dessert felt out of place. Where were my pumpkin and pecan pies? I would have even settled for a gooey slice of fruitcake - anything to feel some hominess for the holidays.

Over the years, I did learn to enjoy some fish dishes, but fixed my way, like baked cod in a mustard and dill sauce. I never did grow to like my mother-in-law's favorite eel dish. For some reason, tuna fish was not very popular in Germany and not available at eateries. It was sold in tins, but already made up in a tomato sauce with onions and peas, not at all like the Albacore I was used to. Crabs were absent from the region and salmon only came smoked.

There were, of course, plenty of other foods to enjoy, especially fresh produce. German housewives tended to shop daily for the freshest vegetables for dinner and buy fresh fruit in season to bake delicious tarts. But I missed certain items like stalk celery – they only had celery root, which had to be boiled – corn, zucchini, and broccoli, which weren't introduced in Germany until years later. Some local produce, like kohlrabi, chicory and white asparagus, which I became acquainted with while living in Germany, have remained among my favorites and I bemoan the fact that they are either impossible to find in U.S. markets, or impossibly expensive.

To be sure, living in a foreign country presented many challenges for me, but I'd venture to say that missing my accustomed food was one of the hardest. When we went on visits to the U.S., which wasn't often, I'd eat my fill of tuna salad sandwiches, crab cakes, corn on the cob and shrimp cocktails with ketchup and horseradish. Even hamburgers tasted better to me in the U.S., maybe because the cattle were fed differently in Germany and the cuts used for ground beef came from different parts of the animal.

Whatever other foods may have seemed lacking during my years in Germany, the magnificent breads, showcased in tantalizing rows, still warm from the oven, made up for it. The irresistible scents wafting from welcoming bakeries would entice you inside, whether you needed bread or not. Large round and oval loaves waited expectantly on the shelves: whole wheat, rye, pumpernickel and multi-grain, so dense you had to have the baker slice them for you, unless you owned a bread slicer and could cut it yourself at home. Of course, the pastries were to die for. After I moved back to the U.S., I could find comparably good pastries, but no baked bread remotely reached the level of tastiness of German bread. To this day, it is the thing I miss most about food in Germany.

Rain in Bremen

*   *   *

THE GRAY SKIES CRIED THEIR bottomless well of tears, making me want to cry sometimes, too. Indeed, I fought weather-induced depression more often while we lived in Bremen than in few other places I've lived. The sun had little chance against the thick wall of water that drenched this northern German town, wedged, as it was, between the North Sea and the Baltic Sea. My husband and I had moved there from southern Germany, where the sun had come out at least occasionally, just enough not to dampen my spirits. In the year we lived in Augsburg, I had grown used to the quirky, changeable weather, influenced by the close proximity of the Alps to the south. Luckily, I was not sensitive to the warm, southern wind, called "Foehn," which came over the mountains into Bavaria and gave many people bad moods and migraines. Still, I missed the frequent sunshine of Maryland.

Bremen was a beautiful city, mostly left intact by the World War II bombs, which, unlike the havoc they wreaked on many other lovely cities, devastated only a few parts of this old port town. By some miracle, the ancient section of town with houses dating back to the 1600's was not damaged at all. The downtown meandered along the Weser River, which was full of flat barges bearing coal and other products northward to Bremerhaven. The misty mornings cast a dreamlike eeriness at times, allowing only the ships' foghorns to penetrate its sodden blanket. For much of the year, the skies were overcast and the winds could be harsh.

People awaited summer with great excitement, hoping it could make up for the typical dreariness, but it could be disappointingly brief, sometimes a matter of only a few weeks, not long enough to restore one's soul. Then, every few years, there would be a surprisingly warm summer with weeks of sunshine and temperatures sometimes topping 80 degrees, which caused some frail people to faint on the streets. They simply weren't used to such heat and no one had air conditioning.

My German neighbors scoffed when I complained about the rain, and told me, in their inimitably practical way, that there was no such thing as bad weather, just improper clothing. People seemed to accept the grayness, even seeing beauty in it. The regional tourist calendars boasted scenes of mist-covered canals, lightly frosted thatched roofs and glistening wet heather. But looking at eye-catching photos of watery charm is a far cry from living in it.

One day, I heeded my neighbors' advice and outfitted myself in high, rubber boots and a long, white raincoat snapped up to my neck. The matching wide brimmed hat made an umbrella unnecessary. I found the same gear for my three-year-old son

Chris, and the two of us headed out into the rain, looking like plastic ghosts slogging through the puddles. It was exhilarating to be able to stroll carefree in the rain while staying bone dry. When I was little, my parents used to call me inside when it rained, probably fearing that I could catch cold. But then, I was prone to illness as a child. Chris, on the other hand, was healthy and active. No matter what the weather, he was always thrilled to be outdoors. On our walks, he collected all manner of rocks and sticks on our path, delighting in their shapes and sizes, not caring that they were sopping wet. Of course, he wanted to drag them all home, and when his pockets were full, he'd stuff mine with his treasures. Rainy days became adventurous days for us.

Peter and I sometimes went to exhibits at local galleries to see paintings by regional artists. Their renditions of rainy landscapes made the subtle tones, like whites, beiges, and charcoal, come alive, such that I started to practice looking at the seemingly barren flatlands around Bremen through an artist's eye. Gradually, and with some effort, they began to look less desolate. Finally, after living in Bremen for several years, I, too, learned to appreciate all the different hues of gray, and to find beauty in their nuances. Even so, I still missed the sun.

The Interview

*   *   *

WHEN WE FIRST MOVED TO the Bremen area, we considered living in town to be closer to Peter's office, but we didn't like any of the rental houses the realtor showed us. I wanted a house with a large yard in a quiet neighborhood away from traffic, where our two-year-old son Chris could play outside. He was very active and needed trees to climb. As an afterthought, the realtor asked if we would like to look at a house in the country, in a village called Leeste, about five miles outside of Bremen. He hadn't mentioned it at first because he assumed that Peter, like most business executives, would want to live in town. As we later learned, it wasn't considered fashionable to live outside the city limits.

I fell in love at first sight with the house on the dusty street named "An der Beeke," which was an old German expression for "on the stream." If there was a stream, I never noticed it, unless the small ditch along the road had once been a wider waterway. The house was a spacious, two-story, three-bedroom brick house with a large fenced in back yard and patio, right next to an open field. The fruit trees and berry bushes reminded me of my grand-father's back yard in Roanoke, where I used to pick black raspber-ries as a child. Peter said he wouldn't mind commuting twenty minutes each way into town to work, probably to appease me. I think he felt guilty for uprooting me from Augsburg, and wanted me to be happy with the place we chose to live.

Leeste was quite rural, populated mainly with farmers who planted feed crops such as rutabagas for their pigs and cows, and sprayed their fields with raw manure. On the days they fertilized, we had to stay indoors with the windows shut. Our street was made of gray cement, not a proper black top pave-ment. A butcher shop, a pharmacy, a bakery, a hairdresser and a post office made up most of the tiny center. For any major shopping we had to drive into Bremen. My neighbors were nice enough, but we didn't have much in common. I became friendly with our cleaning lady, who lived down the street. She was a hearty, no nonsense old-timer, who chided me for crying when our dog got run over in front of our house. She said I should never cry over the loss of an animal.

To most townsmen I must have seemed like an exotic for-eigner, who spoke German with an accent, but they seemed to accept me and tried to make me feel at home. For Chris it was ideal. He went to pre-school in the morning and ran around outside in the afternoon. One day when he was about three years old, I "lost" him in the back yard. Unbeknownst to me, he had climbed up a 20-foot high tree, where I couldn't see him and he didn't hear my calling. To this day, I can't figure out how he did that. Another time, he disappeared from our yard on his tricycle, causing us to panic for over an hour until he was finally found, visiting the hogs in a barn down the road. Chris is still one of the most agile and sure-footed people I have ever met. He does marathons and triathlons routinely and even finished the Iron Man one year.

Through the Cosmopolitan Women's Club of Bremen, I made new friends, but quickly learned that most of them didn't want to drive "so far" out of town to come to my house. I ended up driving to their houses for club meetings. After a while, I started to feel isolated in Leeste and found myself looking forward to the day the cleaning lady came, just for her company. I longed for more intellectual stimulation than "Sesame Street," which I sometimes watched with Chris.

One day, I saw an ad in the newspaper for a bilingual tour guide to show tourists around the old part of town called "Schnoor" - a Middle Low German word for rope maker - that wasn't destroyed by the war, and had newer, arty sections, where jewelry-makers and glass-blowers demonstrated their skills. Peter and I often walked around these areas on weekends, and frequented the pretty cafes. I loved the narrow, cobbled streets lined with squat, crooked buildings from the 1600's that now housed artist studios or galleries. Some of the workshops had large picture windows through which passers-by could watch as the artists painted, sculpted and forged their pieces of art.

If enthusiasm for the town counted for anything, I was sure to be hired. Peter had no objection to my wanting a job, even though it was uncommon in middle class families in Germany at that time for women with small children to work outside the home. Many German women seemed proud of not having to work, and were sometimes identified by their husbands' positions. For example, when we lived in southern Germany, I was referred to as "Frau Doctor Spranger," because Peter had a PhD. Having lived in the U.S., doing an internship for graduate school in economics, he knew that expectations for women's roles were often different in the U.S. than in Germany. He also knew that I liked being independent and was feeling lonely.

The ad said the job would be part-time, several mornings per week, which fit my schedule beautifully. My heart jumped as I carefully read the job description: The person should be college educated, fluent in German and English, and interested in promoting local tourism. The uniform would be provided. The job paid only a small stipend, but I wasn't concerned about the money - I wanted to get out of the house and do some interesting work. I filled out an application, and was called for an interview shortly thereafter.

Even though I knew I met all of the stated requirements for the job, I tried to prepare for the interview by reading up on Bremen's historical and political development, Schnoor's reputation as a center for arts and crafts, and the importance of its site on the Weser River as a commercial and picturesque location.

On the morning of my interview, I stood in front of my clothes closet, still undecided about what to wear, something not too modern or flashy, yet attractive and professional. I chose a blue suit, plain white blouse with a silk scarf and medium heels. My hand trembled a bit as I applied my lipstick. I had never interviewed for a job in German.

I arrived early and sat on the leather couch in the waiting room, trying to calm myself. In spite of my fluency in German, I still got nervous when I had to advocate for myself. It was hard for me to be expressive and appear relaxed, while trying to speak German correctly, all at the same time. Even after years of living there, the grammar didn't come naturally to me, but required an effort in concentration to get the gender of the nouns, and the adjective and verb endings right.

After a few minutes, a man about my age greeted me and ushered me into his office. He asked me general questions, like where I had learned German and how long I had lived in Bremen. When he asked about my qualifications and experience, I answered confidently. I could feel the tension lessening and I smiled more easily. It seemed that the interview was going very well.

As we were about to end, the man asked me, "Oh, by the way, what does your husband do for a living?" This question took me by surprise, since the women's movement in the U.S. had long defined a woman by her own accomplishments, not her husband's, but I knew that concept was still lagging behind in Germany. At social gatherings, I was frequently asked what my husband did, rarely what I did, for a living. In an effort to maintain the pleasant momentum we had reached in the interview, however, I decided to tell the man briefly about Peter's position.

His next question stunned and confused me, "How much money does your husband make?" For a moment I was speechless. What did my husband's salary have to do with this? But I didn't want to jeopardize my chances for the job by alienating him, and I answered honestly. The man raised his eyebrows, cleared his throat and said, "Since your husband earns such a good salary, you don't really need this job. If any problems came up, you would be likely to quit because you don't need the money." With that, he rose from his seat.

I was so flabbergasted, I don't remember what I replied. I'm sure I tried to convince him otherwise, that I seriously wanted the job and would be reliable, but I could tell his mind was already made up. He glanced at his watch, thanked me for coming, and escorted me to the door. I felt awful, like I had done something terribly wrong. Hot tears streamed down my cheek, as I walked quickly to my car.

At home that evening Peter tried to console me, but was upset with me at the same time for giving out personal information about him during the interview. He said the man had no right to ask me questions of that nature, and I shouldn't have answered him. He was right, but I had been blind-sided and hadn't known how to politely refuse to answer. In being too cooperative, however, I had created my own undoing. Of course, nowadays, the whole incident would be called blatant discrimination and I could sue the company. But in those days, there were no such laws. The onus was on me to just say no, but I wasn't so good at doing that then.

Martha Hedwig Gertrud Spranger, 4-06-1902 to 9-18-1984
Peter-Henning Eduard Spranger, 5-31-1931 to 8-04-2009

Trouble Brews

*   *   *

I WISH I COULD SAY THERE were glaring problems in my marriage, like abuse or alcoholism, that led to my leaving Peter, but that wasn't the case. The erosion of our marriage happened slowly, just beyond the edge of my awareness. There were no major incidents that would easily justify my decision to separate from him, but a series of disappointments and disillusionments that collected themselves quietly along the fabric of our daily lives, eventually obscuring the happiness that had once flourished between us.

Our marriage had several strikes against it from the start. We were a culturally mixed couple, living in Peter's country, where I was the "foreigner." I had left my support system, friends and family, and knew only a few people in Augsburg, where we first lived. Peter was trying to establish his career in the supermarket business, which kept him working longer hours with each promotion. His parents lived in Ahrensburg, an eight-hour drive away, and a strenuous trip that they made only seldom. My parents were divorced, and lived an ocean away.

Neither set of parents had knowledge or experience regarding the other's country or customs, which caused a gaping distance between them, not just geographically. Surprisingly, no one ever spoke of the fact that our families had been "enemies" during the war. It just wasn't an issue, as far as I knew.

Even though I spoke German fluently, it was still an effort to speak correctly. and I was determined to speak without an accent, a prideful endeavor that caused me unnecessary stress. Now I know that, unless a person is raised bilingually, it is almost impossible to speak a foreign language with the same ease and confidence as one's mother tongue, much less with no accent.

Peter and I both had troubled upbringings, although for different reasons. He grew up in war-torn surroundings – he was fourteen years old when World War II ended - while I grew up with emotionally-torn parents, both highly unstable situations that caused us each anxiety, but manifested itself in different ways. Peter tended to be high strung while I tended to feel insecure. Sadly, neither of us had any insight about these issues at the time. By default, we blamed each other for selfishness and lack of understanding.

Initially, Peter's parents had tried to welcome me. His father Helmut was thoughtful, even jovial at times, but his mother Gertrud was a serious woman, who seldom smiled. I rarely heard her laugh. Her dark blond hair was always neatly wrapped in a bun at the back of her neck. She was introverted, which I may have interpreted as distant, whereas I was more extroverted and more direct, which may have offended her. She may also have been depressed. Given what she went through, who wouldn't have been? After all, she had suffered unimaginably hard years during the war, which had ended a scant twenty years before we met in 1965.

Gertrud had had to struggle much of the time alone with two young kids, under constant threat of invasion, with air raids jolting their nights, while her husband was away for long periods of time, transporting supplies to the German troops. My father-in-law, like all adult males at the time, had to work for the war effort. If I had been able to appreciate the hardships Gertrud endured, I might have been more compassionate towards her.

Worst of all, in the midst of the war, with practically everything in ruins, Peter's five-year-old sister took ill with meningitis and died. The family had no means to access medication that might have saved her. I don't think Gertrud ever got over her daughter's death. Peter was only nine or ten years old at the time and didn't remember much about it, only that his mother was very sad. By 1944 when the Germans were losing the war badly, boys not much older than Peter were being called up to fight. Born in 1931, Peter just missed being drafted at age thirteen.

I felt sorry that these events had taken place, but had no real understanding of what it was like to live through four years of war in your own country, or how it had negatively affected my parents-in-law, or Peter, for that matter. I was totally naïve about the lingering psychological scars of war, assuming that survivors simply rebuilt their lives and eventually got back to normal. Also, the war seemed so long ago to me – it had ended in 1945 when I was five years old and Peter and I got married in 1966. I now know that 21 years is a mere drop in the sea of time as far as recovering from such a horrendous era. At the time, however, I was more focused on learning to be a wife and adjusting to the German culture.

Since I was already worried about how to fit in, I was especially sensitive to some of Gertrud's remarks. She questioned things I did differently from her, like ways of cooking and doing laundry, possibly out of curiosity, but I took it as criticism. For example, she expected me to serve gravy with dinner, just like her mother and grandmother had done and was shocked to learn that I didn't even own a gravy boat. She thought every vegetable needed a sauce of some kind, made with butter or cream, which I thought was unhealthy. I told her about the move toward lower-fat food that was getting a foothold in the U.S., in part through Adele Davis's books on nutrition, which I read avidly, but she showed little interest, preferring to stick to her traditional ways.

Gertrud was surprised that I didn't iron everything, like underwear and towels, even cloth diapers after Chris was born. I pointed out that ironing those items was unnecessary and a waste of time, but she thought I simply didn't know how to do these tasks properly. I was used to wash-and-wear products and fitted sheets that weren't yet available in Germany. She said if I cleaned up the kitchen as I went, it wouldn't be such a mess when the meal was ready. I resented the implication that I was incompetent. Having learned so much from my mother, I felt confident about running a household, especially since I had lived in some apartments on my own before marriage. While I wanted Gertrud to acknowledge my accomplishments and praise me, she worried that I was doing things incorrectly.

Based on many such misunderstandings, I think my mother-in-law and I each felt rejected by the other. She probably wanted my acceptance just as much as I wanted hers, and must have felt hurt over the contention between us. The main problem as I saw it was that Peter didn't stick up for me. He expected me to accommodate his mother's wishes and disregard my own, not to argue with her, but to understand that she, then in her 50's, was "set in her ways." I wanted Peter to tell Gertrud to accept my different way of doing things. His father was easy going, but also catered to Gertrud, not wanting to displease or upset her. There was little physical affection between them, but he would occasionally poke good-natured fun at her, which she tolerated with patience.

When Peter's parents visited us, Peter wanted me to serve food familiar to them, like roast pork and potatoes, and have meals at the time they were used to eating. They expected the hot meal at noon, followed by a quiet time, usually including a nap, until around 3:30, at which time coffee and cakes were to be served. Afterwards, we sometimes took a walk, weather permitting, or read, wrote letters, or did handicrafts. I knitted or crocheted while Gertrud did wood carvings, painted or wrote children's rhymes. She was an extremely talented woman. By 6:00 pm or so, it was time to set the table for supper, which always consisted of open-faced sandwiches made with cold cuts and cheese, accompanied by pickles and sliced tomatoes. The routine of it all seemed rigid and boring to me, although the predictability was in some ways reassuring.

I didn't realize until later that Gertrud had such high anxiety, most likely resulting from the war years, which would probably have met the present-day diagnosis of PTSD. She was very nervous riding in a car and flinched at loud noises. She could only stand to hear music if it was playing in the background of a mystery story on television, which she loved to watch. She would only go to a certain restaurant, where she would always order her favorite dish, eel in dill sauce. She disliked shopping and never learned to drive. She seemed most comfortable when she knew what to expect. I didn't understand her need for control and considered her habits simply strange idiosyncrasies that she could change if she wanted, rather than attempts to manage her anxiety.

I wish Gertrud and I had been able to accept our differences and look beyond them to appreciate each other's good qualities as people, but I was far too insecure and far too much in need of recognition and approval. Perhaps she was, too. But it wasn't just our relationship that upset me. I felt squelched by the traditional routines of German life in general, as if I were losing part of my self. There wasn't much room for spontaneity or new ideas. If I suggested doing something differently, the response was usually, "We don't do it that way."

Peter had some of his mother's conservative nature, in that he planned things out carefully before executing them. His PhD. in economics helped him land an important position in Bremen in the administration of a supermarket company, probably akin to a vice president in the U.S. He made decisions about which stores in the chain to close, to move or expand. Part of my initial attraction to him was his steadfastness and reliability, in addition to his good looks. He had a responsible job, was educated and cultured, polite and charming, all the traits I found appealing in a man. I didn't realize then how important creativity and spontaneity were to me, believing that stability above all things, which I lacked growing up, would provide me with security and contentment. But Peter tended to follow rules without question and sometimes disapproved of my somewhat daring nature.

One balmy summer evening, Peter and I were taking a walk in the neighborhood. It must have been late June, because some of the fruit trees were already heavy with their offerings. As we walked by a house with a large, fenced garden, I noticed that a branch of their cherry tree was hanging out over the sidewalk, laden with ripe cherries within easy reach. When we came under it, I reached up and picked several cherries and began to eat them. Peter said, "Pat, what do you think you are doing?" I realized right away what he meant because Germans tended to be very protective of their property, but I replied, "What do you mean? I only picked a few cherries." I didn't think it was such a big deal, especially since the branch was hanging over the sidewalk.

Peter proceeded to go into a tirade about how the tree didn't belong to me, how I had no right to pick any of the fruit, no matter where the branches were, and how I needed to respect other people's property. I felt soundly chastised and hurt that he would talk to me in that tone and said, "Peter, you are lecturing me and blowing this out of proportion." We hardly spoke the rest of that night, each entrenched in our respective position. He must have thought I had overstepped unwritten boundaries, which, seen from the eyes of his culture, I probably had, while I felt choked and blamed once again in my desire to be spontaneous.

Another instance when Peter reacted so angrily was the time I took the streetcar without paying. When I realized I had forgotten my purse, I didn't want to get off the tram and walk all the way back home. Payment was under the honor system, whereby passengers were supposed to stamp their pre-paid ticket in a machine when they boarded. There were occasional checks by an official, who would issue a fine to anyone who hadn't paid. I sat quietly with a nervous stomach, eying the swivel doors every time they opened. Luckily, no one checked that day, but when I told Peter about it, he was furious.

He ranted about my dishonesty, and how my actions were unacceptable. He repeated a phrase I often heard people use in Germany: "So etwas macht man einfach nicht," which roughly translates to: "One just doesn't do such a thing." He was yelling and scowling at me over something I thought was not exactly trivial, but certainly not of such importance to cause an outburst. I realize now that Peter may have worried that my behavior, had it come to light, could have reflected somehow badly on him. He seemed to think getting caught would mean some kind of public shame, whereas I would have seen it as simple bad luck and paid the fine like I would a parking ticket. I felt such distance from him when he reacted this way. It seemed like following the rules was more important than my well being.

Thinking back now, I also wonder if, during the war, Peter and everyone else had had to comply with rules and ordinances to the letter, without question, at times perhaps for their very survival. There were curfews, air raids and food rations, for example, that required strict adherence to the rules. Peter never talked much about that period of his life as a young boy and gave vague answers when I asked him about it. His need to follow rules also may have just been a part of his upbringing in the German culture.

There seemed to be many restrictions that affected daily life in Germany, like not walking on public grass, keeping the kids quiet between 1:00 and 3:00 p.m. and not calling a private home during those hours. Saturday morning was often a hassle because the stores closed for the weekend at 1:00 pm, causing a mad dash of people doing their grocery shopping and running errands. One Saturday per month the big department stores downtown stayed open longer, but only until 6 p.m. Nothing was open on Sundays, so running out of milk meant going without until Monday. Even the custom of bringing a bouquet of fresh flowers when invited to someone's house annoyed me, especially if I was running late. I particularly disliked this custom when someone came to visit us, because I'd have to stop in the middle of preparations to look for a vase and arrange the flowers for display.

When we lived in Leeste, people wet-mopped their front stoops and raked the dirt in front of their houses to make even,

orderly lines. Their windows were spotless, flower boxes tastefully arranged, and cars kept shiny. The villagers were mostly
tradesmen, like bakers and butchers, and friendly enough, but
rarely invited us to coffee or dinner, perhaps because we had
little in common. Also, they may have been intimidated by
Peter's position. I liked living out in the country, but it was
lonely at first, trying to make friends and find activities for
Chris. Peter's hours had increased and he was worn out in the
evenings, wanting only to watch television and wind down.
He was also getting migraine headaches more frequently and
had developed a permanent worry line down the middle of his
forehead, which made him look severe.

The Bremen Women's Club was a godsend, consisting
of fellow ex-patriots like me from different countries, most
of whom were married to German men. I made new friends,
played bridge regularly and began to teach English at the Berlitz
School. When we later moved into the city limits of Bremen, I
took in another au pair girl as I had done in Augsburg, both as
help with the house and as company for me.

In 1973, just when Bremen was starting to feel like home to
me, Peter's job was transferred to Hamburg. Since I was highly
pregnant with Linda at the time and didn't want to change
gynecologists, Peter commuted to Hamburg for a few weeks.
On the same day that I was giving birth to Linda at the Red
Cross Hospital in Bremen, Peter and Stefania, our delightful au
pair girl from Jesolo Lido, Italy, were moving us into a duplex
apartment on Leinpfad Strasse on a canal in a lovely part of
Hamburg, called Winterhude. Peter couldn't pick up the baby
and me when we were discharged from the hospital because

of important meetings at work, but sent his newly acquired chauffeur to fetch us instead. The company still held on to some of its old traditions and benefits, such as a car and driver for higher executives. Even though it was exciting to be driven by a chauffeur, I felt sad in the back seat, cuddling our new infant alone. Linda was a gorgeous and delightful baby, who made me very happy, but I longed to share my joy with Peter.

Now living in Hamburg, I was once again torn from the social network I had set up for myself. On top of feeling disoriented in a new place, I promptly developed a mild case of post-partum depression, for which my doctor prescribed an anti-depressant. Since I was nursing Linda, I was reluctant to take it, but she assured me it would not harm the baby. Within a few weeks, I felt better, but couldn't shake the emptiness inside. Peter was stressed and preoccupied in his new position, wanting to do well professionally, and wanting to be a good husband and father, but he couldn't be in two places at once.

I think my mother was living in Hawaii then, remarried for a third time and, from my sister's accounts, probably drinking too much. We didn't think she would be reliable help to the children or me. After we moved to Hamburg, Peter's parents weren't far away, but seemed to need special attention when they came to visit. I didn't know anyone in Hamburg yet, except an old high school friend of Peter's. He and his wife invited us over for coffee one afternoon, as did a couple from Peter's job, which was thoughtful, but I didn't have the sustained support that I needed. When our au pair girl left to return to school in Italy, I felt bereft. She had become like a younger sister to me.

Shortly after we moved into our new place, the washing machine died. For some unknown reason, it took forever for the landlady to get it fixed. To complicate matters, there were problems due to the high water table in the area, combined with a faulty pumping system. Hamburg sits directly on a huge waterway. While waiting for repairs, the chauffeur drove me back and forth to a laundromat, helping me haul dirty clothes into the place, and waiting with me to help fold everything as it came out of the dryer. We took turns keeping an eye on Chris and holding Linda over our shoulders. He was a very nice man, but I wished that Peter could have been by my side as my partner through our domestic crisis.

Then, Chris developed scarlet fever and had to be kept away from Linda for a few weeks until he recovered. It was hard tending to the baby upstairs and trying to keep company with Chris in his room downstairs so he wouldn't feel so isolated. He was very active, probably hyperactive in today's terms, and seemed happiest when swinging on the truck tire hung from a branch of a massive tree in our backyard, or running around, whooping in his Indian headdress. When Peter got home in the evenings, I just wanted a break from child-care and handed the responsibility over to him. I complained to him about feeling neglected, but he didn't see any way to change his heavy schedule. He told me that he didn't punch a time clock and said he thought I was being unreasonable with my expectations. But it seemed to me that every promotion with its new demands on his time and energy was driving us farther apart.

Panic

*   *   *

EVEN AFTER THE POST-PARTUM DEPRESSION subsided, I continued to have plain old depressive flare-ups from time to time. It helped to stay busy or get out of the house. Chris had started first grade, leaving me for much of the day at home with Linda, who was an easy baby. I loved walking her in her carriage along the gorgeous, tree-lined streets of Winterhude. Public transportation was in the form of a ferry that stopped on the canal near our house. I took it once with Linda in her carriage, and window-shopped downtown for a while before heading back. It was an interesting ride, but I felt lonely for adult companionship. We hired a very nice Turkish housekeeper, who came in twice a week. She didn't speak a word of German or English, but was at least some company to me in the house after Stefania left.

Desperate for a task other than housework, I applied for a job teaching feminism at the local college and was crushed when I wasn't chosen. Again, a women's club, The International Women's Club of Hamburg, rescued me. I quickly latched onto the group and agreed to be social chairman, which meant planning get-togethers and outings in and around the city. Finally, I was starting to make new friends and had a mission outside of the house. The club was bilingual, English and German, and did fundraising for charity work, as well as socializing. I felt like I belonged and had an interesting focus, which helped ward off depression. Our book club was lively, especially with some American friends I made, like Lil, who later became an outspoken attorney, and Mary, who went to a Buddhist retreat and returned with a shaved head. Unfortunately, they, too, left with their husbands after job transfers. Lil and I still keep in touch, but we have somehow lost sight of Mary.

In the summer of 1973, when we returned to the U.S. for my high school's fifteenth reunion in Hagerstown, I ran into one of my best friends from tenth grade, Barbara, whom I hadn't seen in years. After we talked for a while, she put her hand on my arm, looked me in the eye and told me that I didn't seem like myself, that I had changed somehow, as if I had lost some of my old spirit. At the time, I wasn't sure what she meant. I thought we had all changed since high school and chalked up her observation as a natural progression of maturation. Looking back now, I think she saw something in me that I had not yet realized. In trying to adapt to my marriage and Germany, I was losing some of my personality and my fun-loving, optimistic self.

I think both Peter and I were overwhelmed with all the changes and new responsibilities in our lives. Neither of us had much support in the way of family or friends to help. We visited back and forth with his parents occasionally, but they were unable to give us much relief as far as baby-sitting. Once, we left the kids with them for a few days, but they were nervous wrecks when we returned, having been afraid that something bad might happen to the kids on their watch. Each of my parents separately, as well as my sister, had visited a few times over the years, but lived too far away to be of any consistent help. Peter and I were usually too exhausted to go out anyway.

Then, after only a year and a half, Peter's company reorganized, giving him new responsibilities back in Bremen and sending us back there to live. At first, I was quite upset, having just found a foothold in Hamburg through the women's club. And, to my surprise, I was beginning to like the big city with all its cultural offerings and opportunities. Up until then, I had preferred smaller towns. I hated the thought of moving again with all its mess and confusion and leaving my new friends, but I tried to focus on seeing my old friends again and picking up with them where we had left off.

Part of my discontent in Germany had to do with my lack of vocational direction. Aside from teaching language classes, which I considered to be mostly a hobby, I missed having a "real" job. I sometimes resented Peter's career. He got to go out into the world each day among interesting people and face exciting challenges while getting paid for his efforts. At least, that's how I imagined his life, while I was stuck at home with repetitive, mundane household chores.

I loved my children, but wanted more intellectual stimulation. So when Linda started pre-school in Bremen, I decided to go back to school myself, this time to pursue a degree in psychology at the University of Bremen, while teaching English to German students and German to foreign students. I also signed up to take classes in psychology at the University of Maryland on the military base in Bremerhaven, hoping to discover ways to feel happier in my life. I knew that I wasn't cut out to be a stay-at-home mom full time and that I needed to get out more and find a vocation for myself.

Peter still worked long hours, which contributed to my loneliness. We kept drifting farther apart, causing me to feel more and more anxious and depressed. If I had known back then that depression can be hereditary, as well as come from the environment, I might not have blamed Peter so much for my unhappiness. I might have looked to my childhood instability and parental dysfunction to understand my needs better and might have learned coping skills to help me meet those needs.

It never occurred to me that my feelings of abandonment could stem in large part from my childhood, with its turmoil and frequent upheaval, including long absences from each parent. I was holding Peter unfairly responsible for much of my discontent.

One day, as I was on my way to Bremerhaven to teach a German class at the American Army base, I felt more nervous than I usually did when teaching German. All of a sudden, the iron sides of the train started closing in on me. As I clutched the arms of my seat, I recognized the familiar signs of an approaching panic attack, but felt helpless to stop it. I stared wide-eyed, but un-seeing, unable to focus. An invisible fist began churning my stomach while a vice squeezed my chest, slowly cutting off my breath. A large, dark amoeba clouded my mind, tangling any hope of rational thought. I could feel beads of perspiration on my forehead.

I wanted to flee, but I was ensnared inside this suddenly unrecognizable body and trapped inside the steel coffin of a train, where I believed no one could hear me even if I could scream. My heart thudded in my throat and chest, threatening to explode. I gasped, but the smothering continued. I felt abandoned, disconnected from the real world, hurtling through a terrifying, Kafkaesque void towards oblivion. I thought I was dying.

After what seemed like an eternity, the panic attack began to subside. I don't know what exactly caused the shift. Maybe this nameless terror had reached its peak, run its course, so to speak, and had to dissipate. Or maybe it was the slowing of the train as it came into the next station, the sound of screeching brakes and a warning whistle - familiar movements and sounds - jolting me out of my nightmare.

As I became aware of my fellow passengers preparing to get off the train and doing everyday things, like reaching for their luggage, draping their coats over their arms, and taking their children's hands, a sense of reality began to return. I heard the reassuring murmur of voices as people lined up near the door to exit the train while other passengers crowded on the platform, ready to board the train. The sight and sound of other people milling around doing normal activities helped re-connect me to the here and now. I breathed a deep sigh of relief that the panic attack had subsided, but felt drained and upset that I still lost control in this manner. I resolved to practice ways to manage my anxiety better in future.

From past experience I knew that if I could catch the early signs of high anxiety, talking to someone right away might help, but the attack seemed to come on suddenly, catching me unawares, as if already full blown and beyond simple interventions. I hadn't realized I was worried about anything in particular until I thought about it later. It was the same old story...

Although I had already lived in the country for years at that point and was quite fluent, I was afraid that a student might ask me a word or phrase I didn't know, or detect an accent. Even though German people said they couldn't tell that I was an American, I wasn't convinced. But then, perhaps my expectations were unrealistic. After all, I hadn't begun to learn German until my sophomore year in college, when my mouth structure was fairly well set. But hadn't I always expected myself to excel in nearly every endeavor I undertook? Being hard on myself was a tendency, which most certainly added fuel to the fire of an anxiety disorder. I was "ehrgeizig," as the Germans would say, which meant ambitious, but with a slightly negative connotation. I wish I had concentrated more on simply communicating with people in German and not worried so much about speaking correctly.

Another way that helped me reduce anxiety was to focus on some detail of things around me, like the intricate weave of a fabric, the patterned grain of wood or pretty color combinations.

Physically holding onto something could also help. At the time, I didn't know why such concrete thinking reduced my nervousness, but now I understand that it shifted the energy from the emotional to the rational side of my brain. Anxiety suspended me in mid air, with no secure footing, while rational thought helped me feel grounded. I've also found that counting backwards or doing rote math, like reciting the multiplication tables, can similarly ward off anxiety, as it puts the focus on logical thinking, which has no room for irrational fears.

I'd had other episodes of anxiety earlier in my life, but it had been a long time since the last one, and an even longer time since one of this magnitude. One of the worst episodes was the time I was flying to Europe for the first time at the age of twenty-one with a group of college students, none of whom I knew, from schools in the D.C. area. I had heard of the opportunity to visit different countries and stay with a German family through the German Embassy.

I was looking forward to the venture and couldn't wait to board the plane, a propeller plane that would take eighteen hours to cross the Atlantic and deposit us in Amsterdam, stopping twice along the way. Jet planes were more expensive and this was a cheaper, charter flight. I felt nervous, too, but thought that was a normal part of the upcoming trip. To add to my excitement, I heard my name announced over the loud speaker at the airport, asking me to come to the main desk. My father had sent me a telegram, wishing me "Bon Voyage," and signed, "Love, Daddy." I was the first person in my family to fly in a plane or travel abroad and he was thrilled for me.

As we waited to board, I met some of the other students, all of whom seemed friendly. But once on the plane, I felt uneasy when I saw the low ceiling, the narrow aisle and the cramped rows of seats, not at all what the airlines showed in their ads. The air was stuffy and storage bins and floor space were quickly overflowing with duffle bags, travel cases, and several guitars. I felt flushed as I sat down in the middle seat and buckled my seatbelt. I introduced myself to Ellen, the student sitting next to me in the window seat, stowed my purse and anxiously waited for takeoff.

The moment I heard the plane's heavy door shut and the large metal handle latched securely in place, a stifling heat rose up my chest into my head, cutting off my breath. As we raced faster down the runway, an overwhelming fear drenched my body, as if I were drowning. When we lifted off the ground, I realized that I was encased in a giant metal box now with no way out. I had never felt this scared or this helpless before. Something made me turn to Ellen and ask her to talk to me. She must have sensed something was wrong and, without question, immediately began to tell me about herself: where she was from, her family, her major at school. In listening to her, my panic began to subside. Then, turning to me and smiling, she asked me about myself. She nodded intently as I spoke and, after a few minutes, I started to relax and smile back at her. It felt so good to breathe freely again.

In the meantime, we had reached our altitude and some of the students were standing in the aisles, talking and laughing, offering each other snacks they had brought along. One person started to play his guitar and others began singing. Someone else brought out a Spanish wineskin full of wine and passed it around. It was the start of what turned out to be a most wonderful trip, in spite of its horrible beginning. I was thankful that Ellen had been so responsive in helping me. She never asked me about what had happened. I wouldn't have known what to say if she had, because at the time, I had no idea what it was, or where it had come from. I only knew that I was shocked and embarrassed about feeling so scared, and I didn't want to talk about it.

The panic attack on the train in Germany had scared me so badly that I went to see a psychiatrist and started taking medication for depression and anxiety, which helped a great deal. Peter and I were bickering often by then, or not speaking at all, except about the children and their needs. My self-esteem had hit rock bottom, and I was feeling unloved and unattractive. My psychiatrist should have realized that Peter and I were having marriage problems that needed couples counseling, instead of treating just me, but at that time marital counseling was not yet widely recognized or practiced as a bona fide treatment in Germany. In fact, it was just beginning to gain significant attention in the U.S.

As part of a requirement in one of my psychology classes in Bremen, I joined a women's support group. It was here, through individual and group sessions that I became aware of how unhappy I was in my marriage. Unfortunately, we didn't explore what role my chaotic childhood might have played in my feelings. I blamed Peter for my increasing bouts of anxiety and began to have thoughts of leaving him. The more depressed and anxious I became, the more I was convinced that I wanted to leave him, but I didn't know whether to stay in Germany or return to the U.S. I knew that uprooting the children would be heart-rending either way and I knew it would be hard trying to manage both of them alone. Still, I assumed they would live with me and was surprised when Peter said they could stay with him. But I would never have considered leaving my children and would have stayed in Germany, had Peter insisted on joint custody. In the end, he left the decision up to me.

During one of our group sessions, my women's group helped me decide what to do. The leader had me face the other members and talk about staying in Germany on my own: where I would live, what I would do and how it would feel. Then she had me do the same thing while thinking about returning to the U.S.: where I would live, what I would do and how it would feel. The group observed me while I answered.

The feedback they gave me was astonishing. Without my realizing it, my demeanor had been completely different during the two exercises. When I spoke of staying in Germany, I looked serious and sounded matter-of-fact as I described how I would find an apartment and get a job when I finished my degree in psychology. But when I spoke of living in the U.S., my face brightened and my voice lifted as I described how life could be for me there, how I would visit old friends and take the kids fun places. The positive energy evident in the latter response had been missing in my life in Germany for a long time. That is not to say that I wouldn't miss my friends and parts of the culture and routine that I had grown to love in the fourteen years I had been there. Certainly, I would miss the satisfying parts of my marriage, but I had lost the motivation to continue facing the difficult parts. I had tried to make a go of it, but my heart just wasn't in it any more. Maybe our personality differences had simply been too great, and the cultural divide too wide to sustain us.

Part Four
Second Chances

*   *   *

Leaving Germany

*   *   *

MOVING BACK TO THE U.S. from Germany in 1979 was harder than I thought and I wasn't ready. The freedom-seeking, adventurous me was still fighting the scared, dependent me, such that I buckled under the weight of the inner turmoil and uncertainty. So, after a summer in Silver Spring, having furnished the house at 204 Parkside Road with our household goods that had travelled across the Atlantic in a container ship, I got cold feet, rented the house out to a young couple and returned to Germany for another nine months. I needed more time to think over my decision.

My German friends welcomed me back and gracefully hid their confusion while saying that they understood. Peter seemed skeptical and kept his distance, but rented a house for us on Hans Thoma Strasse in Bremen. To be honest, I had hoped he would have missed me and been happy to see me again, but he spent most of his time either working or visiting his mother, taking the kids with him on weekends. Neither of us made a move to reconnect with the other. Our relationship was civil, but strained, and lacked any attempt at affection. I think if Peter had tried to woo me again, I might have responded to him and ultimately stayed in Germany, but he seemed even more aloof.

Hoping to strengthen my resolve one way or the other, I started teaching English classes and resumed psychology classes at the University of Bremen. At least I could be investing in a possible future for myself in Germany, should I end up staying. I remained active with my women's support group and continued going to therapy to help sort out my feelings. The anti-depressant I was taking relieved my anxiety a great deal, but I still felt down at times and terribly alone. Thankfully, I wasn't having any more panic attacks. But Peter and I seemed to exist in an irreparable deadlock, in which too many misunderstandings and disappointments had collected themselves, as if a point of no return had been reached. We co-existed under one roof and didn't even discuss the possibility of reconciliation.

Heavy of heart, but more resolved about leaving the marriage this go-around, I said farewell to Peter, my friends and Germany again, this time for good. Since neither of us had tried to revive our marriage, in spite of every opportunity to do so, I felt more confident about my decision now. Nothing had really changed between us since my return, except that I had had more time to digest the truth of our situation. Having once been so in love and believing we could never do anything to hurt one another, it took me that extra time to accept that the flame had truly died.

Packing to leave this time was easier, since many of our belongings were already at the house in Silver Spring. The vision of our furnished house waiting for us was a great comfort. I focused on ways I would decorate it to make a cozy, new home for Linda, Chris and me. As luck would have it, the renters' lease would be up soon, so they would move out just in time for us to move in.

Readjusting in the U.S.

$*$　$*$　$*$

READJUSTING TO THE RHYTHM OF life in the U.S. wasn't a problem. I loved dropping in on old friends, shopping at large supermarkets open around the clock, ordering fast food at the drive-up window, calling people any time during the day and enjoying a feeling of freedom in general. But becoming a single parent was another thing entirely. I hadn't given it much thought beforehand, assuming I could handle things just fine. I had watched my mother do it for varying lengths of time when my parents would separate, but I never paid close attention to how she managed. I remember her looking discouraged at times and complaining about my father's erratic child support, and, even though her secretarial job helped her make ends meet, I knew money was always tight.

Unlike my mother, I wasn't really worried about finances. Peter had promised to send a certain amount of child support every month, based on the German scale for his income, which I assumed would be sufficient, although I didn't really know. After all, I hadn't lived in the U.S. for fourteen years and never with two children to raise. But I felt confident that I could find some kind of work to earn more money if I needed it. Before marriage, I'd always tried to be frugal and live within my means, happy to make do with whatever funds were available. Since my parents were both young adults during the depression era, a time when money and goods were scarce, they seemed to appreciate what little they had and taught my sister and me not to buy things we couldn't afford. Fortunately, I didn't particularly like shopping anyway and had never been interested in acquiring a lot of stuff. Money was a useful commodity, for sure, but not something I worried much about.

In Germany our bills were paid by automatic deduction from our joint checking account, which was funded mostly by Peter's paychecks, but also by mine when I was teaching. Convenient as this system was, it kept me from being informed in any detail about our finances. In addition, I had no knowledge of Peter's retirement account or any investments we may have had. The small income I earned part-time would not have been enough to live on, leaving me financially dependent on Peter and subject to his sense of good will and fairness when we separated.

Since Peter had always been trustworthy, it never occurred to me to ask for a written agreement or any legal document for my protection. Before leaving Germany, I didn't even know what amount I would receive from him each month. Part of my nature has always been to assume that things will work themselves out, which can be both a boon and a bane, depending on the situation. I tend to trust that the future has positive outcomes in store, which sometimes blinds me to possible negative consequences. In this case, I was very naïve and could have been in dire straights, but, thankfully, Peter was an honest and decent man, who kept his word without fail, even paying half of the kids' college tuition many years later.

When my father died in April 1980, he left my sister and me a modest, but nice, inheritance of $25,000 each, with which I bought a small red station wagon and storm windows for the house in Silver Spring, my first major purchases.For the car I negotiated a discount because it had been a demonstration vehicle. At the house the existing casement windows were the old crank-out, single-pane kind that leaked air, raising the electric bill. I was afraid of making mistakes in budgeting my limited funds, but, true to my tendency towards practicality, I thought insulated windows would be a good investment for the future, saving us money in the long run.

To start building at least a small financial cushion, I took a summer job, teaching dance and core subjects like English and math at the Psychiatric Institute, a residential program for kids with emotional problems. The position gave me a taste of institutional mental health work, enough to find out that I didn't like it. Plus, it didn't pay much. I needed to find stable work eventually, but I knew that my master's degree in German and Comparative Literature was not going to land me a job any time soon. For that, I would need a doctorate degree in either German or Comparative Literature, which didn't interest me and wouldn't guarantee me a solid position anyway.

When I was in the midst of fighting panic attacks in Germany, I remember taking a vow with myself to help other people manage their anxiety and depression once I learned how. To this end, I decided to continue studying psychology, which I had started in Bremen, to learn more about the causes and treatment of psychological problems in general, and panic disorder and depression in particular. Most of all, I wanted to get back on that mental horse that had thrown me and take control of the reins, never to feel so helpless again. I was determined to gain the skills and confidence to overcome my insecurities once and for all and, in time, become a psychotherapist for others.

In my teens and early twenties, I remember trying to help my sister when she got depressed, and feeling inept when she said I didn't understand her. My mistake was that I offered too much advice, instead of listening to her feelings. In vain, I tried to convince her to see the positive side of things. She claimed that I hadn't been through the same difficulties growing up as she had, especially with our father, which was true. He had always spent more time me. Maybe because I was athletic and could play sports with him, he could relate more easily to me. My sister's comment that I didn't understand her bothered me. I really wanted to be able to empathize with people's feelings, especially hers, but was apparently going about it in the wrong way. The thought of learning the right techniques to be supportive and effectively help people intrigued me, so I set about finding a way to do it.

Linda and I at International Night
Takoma Park Elementary School

Christian Roger Spranger (14) and Linda Anne Spranger (8)

Returning to Grad School

* * *

WITH SOME TREPIDATION I BEGAN applying to graduate schools in psychology. I worried about keeping up
scholastically after so many years out of school, while managing
all of my new responsibilities as a single parent. When Catholic
University sent me their acceptance letter, I was ecstatic. Finally,
I would be learning a real profession, with which I hoped to get
a good job and accomplish something of value.

As part of my application, I had had to write a statement
explaining why I wanted to study psychology. Leaving out
the part where I hoped to become stronger at keeping my own
anxiety and depression at bay, I focused mainly on my desire
to help other people. At the time, I felt a bit ashamed for not
being totally honest, but in the course of my career, I have yet
to meet a therapist who didn't go into the field of psychology
without a very personal and private reason for doing so, usually
to fight some demon from their past.

Even though I was recovering well and had only occasional,
mild bouts of anxiety and depression, I was sometimes afraid

I might relapse. Strangely, once you have a panic disorder, it is the fear of future panic attacks that is most debilitating, always lurking as a threat. Indeed, even after I had stopped taking the Valium my German psychiatrist had prescribed, I still kept a bottle of it in the medicine cabinet for a long time, well after it had expired, like a security blanket, just in case. Knowing it was there was enough to relax my fear.

On my first day of graduate school in psychology, my heart leapt as I sat with my new notebook and sharpened pencils, awaiting the arrival of the instructor. At first, it felt strange sitting at a student desk after so many years. With most of the other students in their 20's, I could have been their mother and worried about being accepted. But as it turned out, they didn't seem to notice my age and included me easily in the group.

Even though I had always been a hard worker, I found the program quite demanding. Many a late night found me at the dining room table slumped, bleary-eyed, over books on statistics, human behavior and mental illness, much like my mother used to do with her shorthand books after the house had quieted down. Chris used to complain about my mess of papers, even leaving me notes at times, politely reminding me to clean up. It was hard for him to find space for his cereal bowl some mornings. Needless to say, when the first A's and B's started coming in, I exhaled deeply and made more of an effort to keep the table tidy.

Like many other psychology students, I had trouble learning statistics. It made sense during lectures, but I had a mental block when trying to work the problems at home by myself. I met with the teaching assistant as often as I could, practically making a nuisance of myself. One student named Richard had such anxiety about the course that he couldn't even sit inside the classroom. They had to set up a desk for him to sit in the hallway next to the open door, where he could hear the instructor. During break times, I ended up helping him, mostly with encouragement to build up his confidence, but also with the tips the teaching assistant had given me. Thankfully, both of us managed to pass the course.

Juggling house, kids and graduate school by myself taught me the real meaning of feeling overwhelmed. Peter had always pitched in with grocery shopping, fixing dinner and putting the kids to bed. Now, I had to do almost everything alone. Sometimes when I was really low, I had trouble remembering why I had left Peter in the first place. Some pleasant memory would pop up, as if trying to seduce me into questioning my decision. I missed his help, his companionship and the sense I'd had of belonging to a family. But when I remembered Peter's aloofness and my feelings of rejection, the moment of ambivalence would pass. He called occasionally from Germany to check on the kids and me. Once, when I complained to him about how tired I was, he said, "Isn't this what you wanted?"

My mother had moved back to Maryland and helped with the kids for a short while, but started to need my support in ways I hadn't anticipated. One day she took the bus with the kids and got lost on the way back. Luckily, they helped guide her home. Then one evening at dinner, she momentarily forgot how to bring her fork to her mouth. Another time, she couldn't button her blouse. When the doctor diagnosed early onset of Alzheimer's disease combined with mini-strokes, I knew I couldn't leave her alone with the kids anymore. She continued to deteriorate to the point that I felt uncomfortable leaving her unattended, for fear she could leave the stove on or wander outside in the street. Every day I left the house for work, I worried about what I might find when I got home.

Thankfully, I was able to find an assisted living program for her nearby, where she could have her own apartment, receive supervision and help with tasks of daily living in a secure building. She didn't want to move there with "those old people," but it seemed to be a good compromise. We could easily visit her and have her over frequently. It was a relief, knowing that she was safe. But now the kids were alone after school. Actually, at ages eight and thirteen, they were legally old enough to be left alone. Still, I didn't like doing it, but felt I had no choice.

During the first semester at Catholic University, I found out that I could also become a therapist by majoring in clinical social work instead of psychology, and that the University of Maryland at Baltimore offered that degree at a third of the cost. Since money was tight, I promptly transferred and commuted an hour twice per week to Baltimore to class, leaving the kids unsupervised for longer periods of time on certain days. Although legal, it wasn't a good idea. I found out years later that Chris was hanging out with the wrong crowd and Linda was feeling abandoned.

Chris and Linda must have been upset with me for uprooting them from Peter, their friends and Germany, their birthplace, although they didn't talk much about it. I never thought to ask them how they were feeling about all the changes, not realizing how important that would have been. My parents never asked me how I felt about their multiple separations and our many moves and adjustments. In those days, kids were supposed to follow along with whatever their parents did without question and there was little, if any, knowledge about how kids were affected emotionally by their parents' behavior.

I wish I had been more aware of my kids' sense of loss that the move to the U.S. brought with it. I would have encouraged them to express their emotions and empathized with them. Instead, I assumed they were doing just fine in my home-land, where I felt comfortable. Or, maybe they saw me strug-gling and didn't want to add to my burden. It's hard to say, so many things were going on at once. They seemed to be getting used to the American school system and making new friends. Although I had tried to raise Linda and Chris to be bilingual, they must have had some trouble speaking English full time at first, especially at school, but they never said so.

During the first year, I remember feeling exhausted much of the time, trying to manage the house and the kids' school schedules with my own classes, plus the added commute to Baltimore. As nerve-wracking as it was at times with all the assignments and exams, I loved being a student again and looked forward to becoming a therapist and earning a living independently. Some days I felt upbeat, when the kids were getting along and doing their chores and I was finishing a paper for school and had dinner in the oven. Other days I felt discouraged, when the house was a mess and the kids were arguing, my notebooks were sprawled everywhere and dinner wasn't even started yet. I tried to remind myself that other families had good and bad days, too, and it didn't mean I was incompetent or particularly disorganized. Still, with no partner to talk to or share the endless tasks of running a household, I sometimes felt bewildered, wondering whatever made me think I could do this by myself.

One midnight before Easter found me frantically running around at an all-night drug store, putting together the kids' baskets with faux grass, chocolate bunnies and marshmallow chicks. The next morning I got up early to hide neon colored, plastic eggs all around the yard in an effort to keep up all the normal holidays and customs so the kids wouldn't feel deprived. At Christmas, I mingled some of the German customs in with the American ones for old times' sake. The kids especially liked the Advent calendar, opening one window each day during the month of December to reveal a small toy or piece of candy, which they used to do in Germany. They also liked lighting one candle on each of the four Sundays in December until all four candles on the table wreath were lit by Christmas Day. Somehow, Nikolaus Tag on December 6th got lost in the shuffle. The kids and I never could remember to put one of our shoes outside our bedroom door the night before, so Nikolaus could fill them with goodies. Overall though, I thought it important for the kids to remember some of the customs of their birthplace. One time, Linda and I were a big hit when we wore our dirndl dresses to her elementary school's International Night.

In spite of all the challenges, I felt hopeful for the most part and, much like the morning mist lifts gradually in sections, then suddenly reveals a clear, blue sky, my insecurity began to dissipate. Ever so slowly, I felt calmer and more confident, experiencing only occasional tinges of anxiety and depression. The kids seemed to be adjusting well to their new surroundings and I was doing well with my coursework. My dear neighbors were most helpful and made me feel welcome.

Once, when I locked myself out of the house, my neighbor Tim rescued me by climbing up a ladder and crawling into a window on the second floor to unlock the door. I was so grateful that I gave his wife Joann a bottle of White Linen cologne, her favorite. Another neighbor, Paul, gave me a jumpstart when my car battery died. He and his wife Marguerite had the kids over for dinner every Thursday night for a whole semester when I had an evening class until late. Richard, the same person with the statistics phobia, had become a friend. He came over on Linda's birthday to start her party by playing games with about six girls until I could get home from class. My friend Sabrina also helped out, even tutoring Chris when he was having trouble academically. Carol, the mother of Linda's best friend, Danielle, kept Linda many a time when I had other pressing issues, or simply needed a break. What would I have done without such good friends?

Finally, after two years of juggling, scurrying, sweating and fretting, the big day of graduation came in May 1983: I had earned my master's degree in social work (MSW)! Linda and Chris cheered for me from the audience when I walked across the stage with my diploma at the commencement ceremonies at the University of Maryland in Baltimore. I held my head high and couldn't wipe the silly grin off my face. The hard work of finding a job lay ahead, but at least I now had the necessary credentials with which to apply. Back home we threw a big party on our patio to celebrate what felt like a joint achievement of Linda's, Chris's and mine. Without their cooperation and support, I never could have done it.

The Barn
Berkeley Springs, West Virginia

The Barn

*   *   *

AFTER I MOVED BACK TO the States from Germany, Peter signed the country property in Berkeley Springs, West Virginia, over to me as part of our divorce agreement. My scatter-brained idea of creating a health farm and living off the land there with him had long since evaporated as an unrealistic endeavor. We had planned for my mother to stay in the little house on the property, where we could visit her on vacation, but it burned down the first year she lived in it. Although the investigation by the fire chief and insurance agent never determined the exact cause of the fire, it was assumed to have been due to a faulty furnace. Luckily, Mom was not physically hurt, but she spent a week in the hospital being treated for shock.

By the time of the fire, our marriage had fallen apart, so I was faced with the decision of what to do with the property. Peter thought I should keep it for the kids and me to enjoy, or at least as an investment. He figured they would ultimately inherit it anyway. With the house gone, it now consisted of a garage, a shed, and a barn on about thirty acres.

Ever since I had seen a magazine article about someone converting a barn into a cozy house, I had been intrigued by the thought of doing it, too. Back in the early 1980's, such conversions were not as common as they are today. So when I called in two local contractors for their suggestions and estimates, it wasn't surprising that they both discouraged me from trying something so different. They said I should let the barn be a barn, as it was meant to be, and either rebuild the house on its original site, or choose a different site nearby. Although disheartened by their opinions, I couldn't let the idea go.

I began to play with sketches of the barn on graph paper, drawing in squares and oblongs where windows could be, and long spaces where sliding glass doors could open onto a wide deck and a fantastic view. I envisioned rustic rooms inside, leaving the original, reddish brown oak beams exposed between white painted drywall. I thought the kids and I could come there for respite from the city and go hiking, creek walking, and picnicking in the woods.

Before the conversion began, the kids and I spent many exciting weekends of virtual camping at the barn. We had a roof over our heads, but no running water, heat or electricity. We had to carry jugs of water, build fires for cooking, and make pallets of hay for our sleeping bags. The barn's outer walls were made of boards, three to five inches wide, with narrow, open slits between them, so that on clear nights, we could see long, thin strips of stars and clouds. At dusk in the summertime, the fields and meadows sparkled with thousands of tiny fireflies.

We could hear the grating crickets and burping frogs echoing up the valley from the creek. From deeper in the woods, mysterious screeches and whines of unnamed creatures made us catch our breath and clutch our hearts. Somewhere close by, scratching and pattering of small feet punctuated the darkness. If this weren't enough, we would tell each other scary stories to further test our courage. Thunderstorms sent us huddling together, while jolting cracks of lightening and driving rain whipped at our fragile safe haven. Going outside in the darkness to our pre-dug bathrooms was especially challenging. Although we had placed wooden planks on which to balance ourselves over the holes, there was nothing to hold onto, and our flashlights exposed only small circles of safety. We were true pioneers, roughing it in the wilderness. The faint-hearted would surely not survive a deadly spider sting or snakebite!

At daybreak, glowing streams of color would stroke us awake, while cheerful birdsong promised fresh adventures. We trail-blazed and swam in the nearby lake, risking mosquito bites, poison ivy and sunburn. Once, when Chris brought friends along, there was rushing and hiding of "Capture the Flag" across the hillsides, followed by campfire songs and marshmallows under the open sky.

As the construction of our barn-house progressed over many months, we lugged less and less with us to the country. At first, it was a pleasure to see each stage of modern convenience completed. (We clapped and cheered the day the indoor toilet was installed!) But something beautiful was also dying, ever so gradually, hardly noticeably. The floors were covering over the close ties we had felt with the land; the walls were enclosing the air that used to smell so fresh and sweet; the doors were closing out the vibrant sounds of nature. True, we no longer needed candles or flashlights, penknives or matches, but something precious had disappeared. Our pastoral barn was gone, and so was the vibrant, raw country life that it had given us before the builders plied their trade with table saws and drywall buckets.

Confidence Builds

*   *   *

I CAN'T NAME AN EXACT POINT at which I began to feel more confident and content with my new life in the U.S. It was such a gradual process, with one small step leading to the other until the tower of accomplishments began to dwarf the tower of insecurities. My self-esteem had improved greatly to the point that I felt like my old self most of the time. I was even starting to date, which helped me feel attractive and desirable again. Of course, landing my first social work job helped tremendously.

I'll never forget the thrill I felt when the call came, offering me a job as case manager at the Rock Creek Foundation, a psycho-social day program for adults with mental and emotional disabilities. My hand was shaking while holding the phone and I couldn't wait to tell the kids. I had gone to the interview with my left arm in a sling, having fallen off a ladder and fractured my shoulder while sanding the barn door at my place in Berkeley Springs. After Peter had signed the barn over to me, I was fixing it up as a country retreat. I had been afraid Rock Creek might not hire me, since I would be slightly incapacitated for the first several weeks on the job. As it turned out, the program manager only asked me in passing how long I had to wear the sling, but didn't seem very concerned about it. He either liked me or was desperate to fill the position. They were only offering $13,500 per year, but I negotiated for more and settled on $14,000, a rock bottom amount even for social work, which pays notoriously low salaries still today.

After joining the National Association of Social Workers, I wrote a letter to the editor of their newsletter, bemoaning the low salaries for social workers, many of whom have a master's degree and are trying to help some of the saddest, most challenging people in our society. I had hoped to prompt a united outcry across the country, which would lead to at least some improvement of the typical remuneration for the profession. Instead, I received only one reply from another social worker in the next edition of the newsletter. It was a scathing attack, accusing me of being a money-grabbing, selfish egotist, instead of the self-sacrificing, altruistic caregiver that he thought I should be as a social worker. I was flabbergasted. To this day, I see no contradiction in wanting to earn a decent salary while helping people at the same time.

The position at Rock Creek was the first and only social work job for which I had interviewed at the time. Worrying that my broken arm could be an issue at other interviews, I was grateful that this place had accepted me. I reasoned that it was at least a starting point, where I could gain valuable experience to enable me to find a higher paying job later on. Plus, they were willing to hire me before I got my state license. I was afraid to turn it down and risk not finding anything else right away. Per our agreement, Peter had been sending child support every month, but the amount was to be reduced considerably the minute I graduated and was able to look for a job.

Aside from the low salary, Rock Creek was a great place to learn casework. I had a variety of clients with wide ranging problems, such as developmental delays, physical handicaps, seizure disorders, autism and mood disorders, all of which would see me in good stead when I would open my own practice. Some of the clients, however, were unpredictable. One day at work, a client with anti-social tendencies suddenly came towards me and shoved me hard to the floor. I wasn't physically injured, but the shock of his assault stayed with me for weeks afterwards. Apparently, I had walked too close to him when leaving a room and he had felt threatened. From that experience, I learned to be more vigilant. Also, I decided I didn't want to work with such severely disabled people.

During the year I worked at Rock Creek, I learned something else important about myself: I didn't like being a team player. It was difficult for me to admit it to myself at first, because being a team player seemed to be a common expectation of social workers, almost a necessary character trait, so to speak. But a team approach meant long, interdisciplinary staff meetings with professionals expressing their various opinions regarding clients' goals and progress, which would make me squirm in my seat, longing to get on with it. In private practice I would be able to work independently and have more control over my workday. As needed, I could arrange for peer supervision and guidance regarding my clients. But first, before I could even work as a certified social worker anywhere, I had to complete 2,000 hours of supervised social work and then pass the state licensing exams.

To help meet my licensing requirements and to earn some extra money, I took a part-time job working as an office assistant for a psychiatrist named Jeffrey, who said he'd also let me do therapy with some of his uninsured clients under his mentorship. It seemed like a good arrangement, but it turned out that I never knew what I would find when I came in to work.

Jeffrey lived with his gay partner in a narrow townhouse in Georgetown, where he saw clients after his day job at a hospital. They sometimes bickered with each other, mainly about the long hours Jeffrey was working. I would come into the office on some afternoons to find terse notes they had written to each other and put around the house, apparently since they weren't speaking. My boss would sometimes call me and ask me to leave a message for his partner, who would react angrily and request that I send a snippy retort back to my boss.

It was always lively and often amusing at their house, but keeping proper boundaries was practically impossible. My work desk was divided from their bed only by a tall screen five feet away. When the two of them had had dinner parties until late, my boss would sometimes ask me to clean up the living room, or put the dishes away, or put the sofa bed back together in the therapy room the next day. After the first few times, I put my foot down and told him these tasks were not in my job description. Since he had been encouraging me to be more assertive in collecting payments from health insurance companies, he didn't seem to mind my becoming more assertive with him. In any case, he took it well and we maintained a good relationship. After all these years, he still sends me a calendar every New Year's. During the year I worked for him, I learned many ins and outs of running a private practice, which would come in handy when I opened my own office one day.

Once I passed my exam to become a full-fledged licensed clinical social worker, I got a full time job as case manager in Child Welfare Services with Montgomery County, mainly for security and benefits. With a master's degree the starting salary was a meager $25,000 per year, not much for the level of education and responsibility the position required, but I had never earned so much money before and was elated. Unfortunately, long staff meetings were again the norm, along with mountains of bureaucratic paperwork. But I saw it as temporary, since my real dream was still to have my own private practice and be my own boss.

To supplement my income and gain more experience doing therapy, I took a part-time job working evenings for an employee assistance program, called "Human Affairs International." It was there that I met Lauri, a fellow social worker, who has "rescued" me innumerous times when I hit dead-ends with paperwork – never my strong suit – and supported me when I felt particularly challenged by some of my clients' issues. At this job I saw individuals, couples and families with problems such as relationship issues, stress, grief, anxiety and depression. I did assessments, referrals and short-term treatment, which I found challenging and stimulating. I loved brain storming with my clients about ways to lessen their stress and find more life satisfaction. I liked the creativity and autonomy afforded by working on my own, which further cemented my desire to have my own business.

Love Seats

* * *

AFTER WE MOVED TO HAMBURG, Peter and I went to the furniture store to buy a matching pair of love seats. I liked their cozy shape and soft velour upholstery. He liked their elegant, yet modern look and their dark color. We placed them across from each other, with Peter's sleek, glass coffee table between them in the large, sunken living room of the house Peter had just rented for us. The arrangement was stylish and fit nicely in front of the stately, granite fireplace.

The expansive room had plush, cream-colored wall-to-wall carpeting, which skirted the white walls. It was an airy space with high ceilings, full of large picture windows, and overlooked a smoothly groomed lawn. Peter's large black leather sofa stood on one wall and was flanked by gold and black coach lamps. I never sat there, but admired it from a distance. Leather felt cold to me, and unyielding, even as I was intrigued by its European look. Actually, I didn't spend much time in that living room, except to entertain guests, but preferred to sit at the kitchen table.

When our marriage ended after fourteen years, I brought the two love seats to the U.S. with me. They travelled across the ocean in a container ship with other items I chose to keep from our time together. Peter kept his leather sofa. One of the love seats I took to my barn in Berkeley Springs. It was one of the first pieces of furniture to find its home in this rustic weekend house. The little sofa was transformed from its earlier, more elegant life in Germany to suit its simpler surroundings when I had it slip-covered in a peach-colored denim fabric. It is faded now and has a broken leg from so much use, but can still stand if supported by a block of wood on one side.

I used to rent my country getaway, as I called it, by the weekend to people who wanted to relax in the peaceful atmosphere of the countryside. Since we made all the arrangements over the phone, I never met most of them in person. I liked to imagine them sitting on the love seat to admire the view of the rolling meadow bordered by woods on either side with the purple mountains in the distance. I wondered if they watched the magnificent sunsets from this spot, as I did when I spent time there. Perhaps they liked to unwind on the little sofa, reading, or knitting, or just warming themselves by the wood-burning stove. They may have seen a screech owl winging overhead, or a family of wild turkeys strutting across the meadow in broad daylight, or deer grazing at dusk. I hope they found contentment, sitting in front of the sliding glass doors so close to nature. The view from this love seat has always had a calming effect on me.

The other love seat still wears its original velour dress, though worn now after all these years. Its seat cushions are missing some of their buttons. It stands in my therapy room in my home office in Silver Spring, where my clients sit on it and pour out their worries in the safety of its warm, fuzzy arms. When I see them supported by this love seat, I am reminded of the transformation I have experienced since leaving Germany. It was hard at first, but I adjusted in time. When my clients are going through difficult changes, I try to reassure them that they can find their way back to a more stable, happier life. I encourage them to live each day, to do the best they can, and to have hope. I tell them that life moves along, takes surprising turns and inevitably leads us to the next thing, the next challenge, career, or partner, which promises new moments of joy. I know this. I've been there.

I have made peace with my divorce, even though it still hurts sometimes when I let myself think about it. We were so much in love when we bought those sofas together. What became of that wonderful loving feeling? How could it erode as it did? It happened ever so slowly without our noticing in time to stop it. It was a sad chapter in my life, but many happier chapters have been written since then.

These two love seats are important markers of my life. They could tell a story of my self-doubt, sense of failure and fear of loneliness. They could describe how I slowly rebuilt my life, recovering my self-esteem and pursuing new goals. One of them has witnessed the barn becoming a healing retreat; the other has seen my private practice develop over the years. In addition to providing my livelihood, the retreat and my practice have provided meaning in my life. I like to think that both endeavors have helped alleviate at least some measure of pain in the world. The sofas provided me solace as I transformed my life and they continue to provide comfort for others.

Aster, Linda and Chris
Silver Spring, Maryland

Second Chances

* * *

Although I'm glad I took the plunge to start a new life for myself by leaving Germany, I was plagued with doubts off and on for quite a while. When Peter and I got married, I had taken my wedding vows very seriously, but we hadn't been happy for a long time and I saw no way to change that. I had felt stifled and wanted a second chance to flourish in life. My goal was to recapture some of that self-confidence and contentment I remembered having before I got married.

I knew I'd have to continue wrestling with my fears along the way, but they no longer held the power to paralyze me as before. The experience of learning to manage my anxiety fortified my belief in myself. The last thing I wanted was to look back one day and regret having allowed my anxiety to control me. I was able to make decisions and take action, even when something scared me. If I made the first move, I felt confident that a new path would open up in front of me and lead in a positive direction.

While life rarely provides guarantees, I believe it does provide an ongoing stream of opportunities, there for the pursuing. The very act of leaving Germany and returning to the U.S. meant giving myself second chances. I fulfilled that promise by establishing a new home for myself and my kids, by going back to graduate school and by building a career for myself.

How did it all turn out? Did I find the peace and contentment I craved? With a few reservations, given life's normal ups and downs, I can answer yes to both questions. This is not to say that I haven't second guessed some of my decisions or wondered what would have happened if I had chosen a different path. But I believe I did the best I could with what I knew at the time. Leaving the marriage when I did was the right decision. Sure, I wonder whether we could have salvaged our relationship if we had received the right help and guidance. Perhaps, but there was probably already too much hurt and resentment in our hearts.

Though I later missed certain aspects of living in Germany, life in the U.S. suited my personality much better. I had disliked being the foreigner, the one expected to make the adjustments and fit in. As soon as we got back to the U.S., I felt more at home, more open and hopeful that there would be good opportunities for the kids and me. However, being a single parent was challenging at best and very frustrating at times, much harder that I had anticipated.

In spite of my sometimes bumbling attempts to raise Chris and Linda, then later Aster when she came to live with us as a foster child, by myself, I think they have all turned out very well. But I wish I had known more about good parenting and had understood their feelings better. At least I felt more comfortable raising them in the States in my own culture. They are caring, responsible people, who have meaningful relationships and are passionately engaged with life. They seem to be happy, which makes me happy. I love them to death and am awfully proud of them.

Becoming a psychotherapist was the right career choice for me, and, looking back, I can see how some of my early life experiences helped pave the way in that direction. For example, growing up in a household with frequent, sometimes violent, arguments sparked my desire to find out how other people live in harmony. Wanting to understand why the neighbors didn't try to stop my father's rage led to my interest in human behavior. Trying unsuccessfully to help my sister feel better when she was sad made me resolve to learn more about the causes and treatment of depression. Realizing that simply listening to my father with compassion when he cried on my shoulder the night he told me he was leaving taught me the power of consolation. Then there was the phone call with the man who had a bizarre fetish about women's footwear, which made me wonder how to help him. And my grandmother Mildred's paranoia and shocking decline gave me some insight about mental illness. Finally, the agony of my own panic attacks fueled my determination to understand their cause and to overcome them.

Studying clinical social work gave me the skills to help people and taught me more empathy towards myself and others.

I learned about different personality types and the reasons why people do what they do, which helped me understand and accept my family, friends, clients, and myself better. My experience with anxiety taught me to be more understanding of other people's vulnerabilities and more patient with their idiosyncrasies.

Today, even after many years as a therapist, I continue to find the work very interesting and challenging. I believe I have provided some measure of comfort and help to my clients, most of whom I genuinely like. In listening to their life struggles, I often recognize some aspect of myself and feel confirmed in our shared humanity. We are not so different from each other after all. I assure my clients that they can have second chances if they are willing to make some changes and take some risks. I know. I did it. I remind them to express their feelings, accept themselves and speak up for what they want and need. By hearing myself give them words of encouragement, I benefit as well. In trying to practice what I preach, I help sustain myself.

When I said I wanted peace in my life, I meant an emotional peace, which I find takes ongoing practice. Yoga, meditation, walks in nature can all help, but it is not a state we can reach once and for all. For example, I have to remind myself to stop and rest when I'm tired rather than push through and end up exhausted. Sometimes in the afternoon, I try to meditate during a break between clients to help me stay grounded. Just being still and practicing deep breathing is calming and refreshing, but I don't do it regularly enough. Either the phone rings or the dog scratches at the door to be let in. To block out noise, I've recently purchased high quality earphones, which work wonders. Sometimes I use an app on my phone for a guided meditation with relaxing nature sounds, which I can set for any length of time. I find that as little as five minutes of solitude can be refreshing and make a difference.

Since my tendency is to stay active and get things done, it's not easy to slow down, even when I know it's good for me. At a party I'm likely to be the one carrying dishes for the hostess, rather than relaxing or socializing. It is satisfying for me to see tangible results of my actions. Also, keeping busy has sometimes been easier for me than meeting new people. Due to my apparently extroverted tendencies, no one would suspect that I'm really a bit shy and self-conscious at times.

Over the years, I've learned that a good measure of serenity is important for me to feel balanced, which means I need to be alone as much time as I need to be with other people. I've had to learn to set limits on other people's requests, so as not to become physically or emotionally depleted. In reminding my clients to be aware of their needs and take care of themselves, I remind myself to do the same.

I've written this memoir to try to make sense of my life and to help my kids know who I am as a person. Growing up with someone doesn't necessarily mean you understand who they are as people in their own right. When you're a child, your focus is naturally on your own universe. Through writing about my parents, I believe that I know them better now. They were people who simply tried to live their lives as best as they could with the knowledge and skills they had. While acknowledging their limitations, I can appreciate their good intentions and forgive their shortcomings. I hope that my kids can do the same for me, once they know my story.

My life experiences have taught me that it's better to take a step into the unknown towards a chance for more fulfillment than to stay with the known and be discontent. Opportunities are around every corner if we have the courage to step towards them. We need to follow our intuition and trust that things will work out, knowing that the majority of people are decent and will help us if we ask. I've learned that most people are much like ourselves, just doing the best they can and are mainly brave and lovable, especially when we know their life stories.

Linda, Chris and I

Acknowledgements

* * *

I'D LIKE TO THANK MY husband Gerry for his endless patience in helping me maneuver the computer when I would get lost with confusing operations and not find my way out. Without his support, I would have succumbed to the virus of frustration that attacks people who are not mechanically minded. He also took on the lion's share of dog-walking and dinner-making to give me extra time to write.

Enormous thanks and appreciation go to my writing mentor, Janice Gary, who came to my house over many months to pore over my rough drafts with me and whip them into literary acceptability. She was also the first person to tell me that, in looking at all the separate pieces, she saw a book in the making. When my motivation occasionally waned, she encouraged me to press forward. Bless her.